ASIAN COOKBOOK FOR DIABETICS

Healthy and Delicious Recipes to manage Diabetes and enjoy the flavors of Asia

By

Ruth R. Crawford

Copyright © by Ruth R. Crawford 2022. All rights reserved.

Before this document is duplicated or reproduced in any manner, the publisher's consent must be gained. Therefore, the contents within can neither be stored electronically, transferred, nor kept in a database. Neither in Part nor full can the document be copied, scanned, faxed, or retained without approval from the publisher or creator.

Table of Contents

Introduction 6
Chapter 1 8
Basic Nutrition for Diabetic Cooking 8
Understanding the Basics of Diabetes and Nutrition 10
Analyzing Foods for Diabetics 11
Understanding Carbohydrates and Glycemic Index 13
Chapter 2 15
Asian Cooking Basics 15
Utensils and Equipment used in Asian Cooking 16
Techniques, Tools and Ingredients of Asian Cooking 17
Popular Asian Herbs and Spices 18
Chapter 3 21
Recipes 21
Soups 22
Vegetable Miso Soup 22
Egg Drop Soup 24
Hot and Sour Soup 25
Chicken and Rice Soup 27
Vegetable Soup 29
Clear Mushroom Soup 31
Bamboo Shoot Soup 33
Vegetable Broth Soup 35
Tofu and Vegetable Soup 37
Coconut Milk Soup 38
Spinach and Tofu Soup 40
Chinese Celery Soup 42
Burdock Root Soup 44
Broccoli and Mushroom Soup 45
Japanese Pumpkin Soup 47
Seaweed Soup 49
Chinese Cabbage Soup 50
Winter Melon Soup 52
Sweet Corn Soup 54
Carrot Soup 55
Bok Choy Soup 57
Chinese Spinach Soup 59
Hot and Sour Fish Soup 62
Tomato Soup 64
Chicken Noodle Soup 66
Udon Noodle Soup 68

Wakame Soup 70
Miso Eggplant Soup 71
Bok Choy and Tofu Soup 73
Side Dishes..75
Stir-Fried Bok Choy with Garlic and Ginger 76
Spicy Eggplant Stir-Fry 77
Cabbage and Tofu Stir-Fry 79
Asian-Style Cauliflower Rice..80
Rice Noodle and Vegetable Stir-Fry 82
Chinese-Style Baked Vegetables..84
Low Carb Asian-Style Coleslaw 86
Steamed Edamame with Soy Sauce..88
Baked Asian-Style Eggplant...89
Miso-Glazed Eggplant...91
Steamed Bok Choy 93
Grilled Tofu and Vegetables...94
Asian-Style Asparagus and Mushrooms 96
Sesame-Ginger Broccoli...97
Asian-Style Green Bean Salad 99
Stir-Fried Spinach with Garlic..100
Asian-Style Cucumber Salad..102
Tofu and Vegetable Lettuce Wraps 103
Sweet Potato Fries with the Asian-Style Dipping Sauce.......................105
Grilled Eggplant with Miso Sauce 107
Grilled Asian-Style Squash 109
Asian-Style Marinated Tofu 111
Stir-Fried Chinese Broccoli 112
Grilled Tofu and Peppers..114
Asian-Style Quinoa Salad...115
Asian-Style Tomato and Cucumber Salad...117
Asian-Style Egg Drop Soup 118
Asian-Style Cabbage and Potato Soup...120
Asian-Style Noodle Soup 122
Main Dishes..124
Vegetable Stir-Fry 126
Brown Rice Bowl with Vegetables 127
Tofu and Veggie Pad Thai..129
Egg Drop Soup 131
Sushi rolls with cucumber, avocado and pickled ginger 133
Grilled Fish with Steamed Vegetables 135
Vegetable Fried Rice 137
Chicken Teriyaki with Steamed Vegetables..139

Miso Soup with Tofu, Seaweed, and Mushrooms 140
Vegetable Lo Mein 142
Grilled Chicken and Vegetable Skewers 144
Thai Yellow Curry with Vegetables 146
Chicken and Vegetable Tempura 148
Vegetable-Filled Egg Rolls 149
Vegetable Ramen 152
Sesame-Crusted Salmon with Steamed Vegetables 153
Sweet and Sour Stir-Fry 155
Grilled Vegetables over Brown Rice 157
Japanese-Style Omelette with Vegetables 159
Steamed Dumplings with Vegetables 161
Korean-Style Beef and Vegetable Stew 162
Vegetable Curry 164
Vegetable Spring Rolls 167
Egg Foo Young 168
Grilled Shrimp and Vegetable Skewers 170
Stir-Fried Noodles with Vegetables 172
Korean-Style Stir-Fried Glass Noodles 174
Vegetable-Filled Steamed Dumplings 175
Tofu and Vegetable Stir-Fry 177
Vegetarian Sushi Rolls with Cucumber and Avocado 179
Desserts 180
Coconut Jello 182
Coconut Rice Pudding 183
Red Bean Soup 185
Mango Pudding 187
Sweet Potato Pie 188
Tapioca Pudding 190
Rice Pudding with Sesame Seeds 192
Sesame Balls 194
Almond Cookies 196
Matcha Pancakes 197
Steamed Buns with Sweet Bean Filling 199
Chinese Egg Custard - Diabetes-Friendly Recipe 201
Fried Banana Roll 203
Fried Dough Sticks 204
Caramelized Apples 206
Baked Sweet Potatoes 207
Baked Sweet Potato Balls 209
Fruit Compote 211
Date-Walnut Cake 212

- Baked Apples with Cinnamon 214
- Baked Sweet Potato Mash 215
- Fried Tofu with Syrup 216
- Fried Taro Balls 218
- Black Bean Soup 220
- Sweet Red Bean Soup 221
- Sesame-Honey Glazed Apples 223
- Baked Rice Cake 225
- Sweet Rice Cakes 227
- Chinese Sesame Balls 228
- **Conclusion** 231

Introduction

Susan had a passion for Asian food. She was always excited to try out new recipes and her friends often raved about her cooking. Unfortunately, Susan also had diabetes and had to carefully monitor her diet to keep her health in check. One day, Susan was browsing the shelves of her local bookstore when she stumbled across my book "Asian Cookbook for Diabetics". She was intrigued and decided to buy the book. My book contains a variety of recipes that are both delicious and diabetes-friendly. Susan was delighted to find recipes for her favorite dishes, like Tofu and Veggie Pad Thai and Vegetable Fried Rice. She was also pleased to find that all of the recipes included nutritional information, so she could easily calculate how many carbs she was consuming with each meal.

Susan was amazed at how easy it was to follow the recipes and how delicious the food tasted. She was also happy that she could enjoy her favorite dishes without worrying about her diabetes. As the months went by, Susan continued to cook delicious Asian dishes while keeping her diabetes in check. She even began to share her recipes with her friends and family. Everyone was amazed at how delicious and nutritious the food was. Susan was so happy that she had found a way to enjoy her favorite cuisine while managing her diabetes. She often thought back to the day when she found the Asian Cookbook for Diabetics and thanked her luck for finding such a helpful resource. Thanks to my book, Susan was able to continue to enjoy her favorite Asian dishes while keeping her health in check.

Diabetes is a condition that affects millions of people around the world. It can be especially difficult to manage when you are trying to maintain a healthy diet. This cookbook is designed to help make it easier to eat healthfully while enjoying the unique and delicious flavors of Asian cuisine. With over 100 recipes, you can explore the wide variety of flavors that make up the diverse culture of Asian cuisine, from spicy curries to fresh salads. Whether you are looking for a quick snack or an elaborate meal, this cookbook offers something for everyone. Each recipe is designed to be low in sugar and packed with healthy ingredients to help you manage your diabetes while still enjoying the delicious flavors of Asian cuisine. So, come join us in the kitchen and let's explore the wonderful world of Asian food!

Chapter 1

Basic Nutrition for Diabetic Cooking

Diabetic cooking is a form of cooking that is specifically designed to help diabetics manage their diabetes. It focuses on providing balanced meals that are low in fat, carbohydrates and sugar, while still providing necessary nutrition. Eating a healthy, balanced diet is important for everyone, but it is especially important for people with diabetes as it can help to control blood sugar levels, reduce the risk of complications and ensure that all essential nutrients are being met. This essay aims to provide an overview of basic nutrition for diabetic cooking and how to ensure a healthy and balanced diet. The first step to creating a diabetic cooking plan is to understand the basics of nutrition.

It is important to ensure that the foods chosen are nutrient dense, providing essential vitamins and minerals that are necessary for health. This includes eating plenty of fruits and vegetables, lean proteins, healthy fats, and whole grains. These foods should be low in sugar and fat, but still provide essential nutrients and fiber. It is also important to be aware of the glycemic index of the foods being consumed. The glycemic index is a measure of how quickly a food can raise blood sugar levels. Foods that have a high glycemic index, such as white bread and potatoes, should be avoided or limited as much as possible. Instead, opt for low-glycemic foods such as whole grains, legumes, and non-starchy vegetables.

Additionally, it is important to include healthy fats, such as olive oil and avocados, as these can help to reduce the glycemic index of a meal.

Another important aspect of diabetic cooking is portion control. Eating smaller portions can help to maintain blood sugar levels and prevent overeating. Eating three meals a day, with two to three snacks in between, is a good way to ensure that all essential nutrients are being met and that hunger is kept at bay. It is also important to be mindful of the types of food being consumed, as some foods may contain high amounts of sugar or carbohydrates. Finally, it is important to ensure that all meals are balanced. A good way to do this is to follow the plate method, which recommends that half of the plate is filled with non-starchy vegetables, a quarter of the plate is filled with lean protein, and the other quarter is filled with a whole grain or starchy vegetable.

This ensures that all essential nutrients are being met, while still keeping blood sugar levels in check. In conclusion, diabetic cooking is a form of cooking that is designed to help those with diabetes control their blood sugar levels and maintain a healthy, balanced diet. The key to successful diabetic cooking is to ensure that all meals are balanced, with plenty of nutrient-dense foods, keeping sugar and fat intake to a minimum. Additionally, it is important to be aware of the glycemic index of foods, as well as portion control, in order to ensure that all essential nutrients are being met. By following these basic guidelines, it is possible to create a successful diabetic cooking plan that is both healthy and delicious.

Understanding the Basics of Diabetes and Nutrition

Diabetes is a serious medical condition that affects millions of people worldwide. It occurs when the body is unable to produce enough insulin, or when the body does not use the insulin it produces properly. This leads to high levels of sugar in the bloodstream, which can cause a variety of health problems. In order to effectively manage diabetes, it is important to understand the basics of diabetes and nutrition. The first step in understanding diabetes and nutrition is to understand what diabetes is and how it affects the body. Diabetes is a disorder of the body's metabolism, or the way the body processes food. In people with diabetes, the body either does not make enough insulin or does not use the insulin it makes properly. Insulin is a hormone that helps the body use glucose, or sugar, from food for energy.

When the body does not produce enough insulin or is unable to use the insulin it produces properly, glucose builds up in the bloodstream, leading to high levels of sugar in the blood. High levels of sugar in the blood can cause a variety of health problems, including heart disease, stroke, kidney disease, and nerve damage. People with diabetes must carefully manage their condition in order to avoid these serious health complications. One of the most important ways to manage diabetes is through proper nutrition. Proper nutrition is essential for people with diabetes. Eating a balanced diet that is low in fat, sugar, and salt, and high in fiber and complex carbohydrates is key to managing blood sugar levels.

Some foods that are particularly beneficial for people with diabetes include whole grains, fruits, vegetables, lean proteins, and low-fat dairy products. Eating smaller, more frequent meals throughout the day can also help to regulate blood sugar levels. In addition to eating a healthy diet, people with diabetes should also be sure to practice portion control. Eating too much food can cause blood sugar levels to spike, so it's important to be mindful of how much food you're eating. Finally, it's important to stay physically active. Regular physical activity can help to regulate blood sugar levels and reduce the risk of developing other health complications associated with diabetes.

Understanding the basics of diabetes and nutrition is essential for people with diabetes. Eating a healthy diet, practicing portion control, and staying physically active can all help to manage blood sugar levels and reduce the risk of developing other health complications associated with diabetes. By following these guidelines, people with diabetes can lead healthy and fulfilling lives.

Analyzing Foods for Diabetics

Analyzing Foods for Diabetics is an important way to ensure that diabetics are able to maintain their blood sugar levels. Diabetes is a chronic disease that affects the way the body processes blood sugar. People with diabetes must carefully monitor their blood sugar levels to ensure they remain within a healthy range. This can be done through diet and exercise, but it is also important to analyze the food a diabetic person is consuming. By analyzing the food, a diabetic can make sure that they are eating foods that are healthy for them and not those that could potentially cause a spike in their blood sugar levels. When analyzing food for diabetics, it is important to consider the nutrition facts. The nutrition facts will provide detailed information about the amount of calories, carbohydrates, fat, protein, and other nutrients found in the food. It is especially important to look at the amount of carbohydrates in the food, as carbohydrates are the main source of sugar in the body and can cause a spike in blood sugar levels. Additionally, looking at the glycemic index of a food can also be helpful. The glycemic index is a number that measures how quickly a food is broken down into sugar and absorbed into the bloodstream. It is also important to look at the type of carbohydrate a food contains.

Simple carbohydrates, such as those found in processed foods and sugary drinks, are digested quickly and can cause a large spike in blood sugar levels. Complex carbohydrates, such as those found in whole grains, fruits, and vegetables, are digested more slowly and can help to prevent large spikes in blood sugar levels. When analyzing foods for diabetics, it is also important to consider the portion size. Eating too much of even a healthy food can cause a spike in blood sugar levels, so it is important to be aware of the portion size and not eat too much. Additionally, it is important to look at the ingredients list and avoid foods with added sugars and artificial sweeteners, as these can also cause an increase in blood sugar levels.

Finally, it is important to keep in mind that foods are not the only factor that affects blood sugar levels. Exercise, stress, and medications can all affect blood sugar levels and should be taken into consideration when analyzing foods for diabetics. By carefully analyzing the food a diabetic person is eating and taking into consideration all of these factors, they can make sure their blood sugar levels are within a healthy range and that they are eating a nutritious and balanced diet.

Understanding Carbohydrates and Glycemic Index

Carbohydrates are essential to our diet and provide us with energy to help us function throughout our day. However, not all carbohydrates are created equal. The glycemic index (GI) is a tool used to measure the relative impact of certain foods on our blood sugar levels. Understanding carbohydrates and the glycemic index is key to making good food decisions and maintaining a healthy lifestyle. Carbohydrates are the main source of energy for our bodies and come in three forms: sugar, starch, and fiber. Sugars are the simplest form of carbohydrates and provide quick energy.

They are found in fruits, vegetables, and dairy products. Starch is a complex form of carbohydrates and provides sustained energy. It is found in grains, such as wheat and rice, and also in potatoes and legumes. Fiber is indigestible and can help slow down the digestion process, which helps to regulate blood sugar levels. It is found in whole grains, fruits, and vegetables. The glycemic index rates the effect of different types of carbohydrates on our blood sugar levels. Foods with a low GI are those that cause a slow and steady rise in blood sugar levels. These are usually complex carbohydrates and should be the focus of a healthy diet. Foods with a high GI cause a rapid rise in blood sugar levels.

These are usually simple carbohydrates and should be eaten in moderation. It is important to understand how carbohydrates and the glycemic index work together to help us make good food choices. The glycemic index can help us determine which foods are good for us and which ones should be eaten in moderation. Eating a diet that is low in simple carbohydrates and high in complex carbohydrates can help regulate our blood sugar levels and provide us with sustained energy throughout the day. When selecting foods, it is important to look at the glycemic index and choose foods with a low GI. Foods that are high in fiber are usually good choices, as they have a low GI and can help regulate blood sugar levels.

It is also important to limit the amount of sugar and simple carbohydrates that we eat. Eating too much sugar and simple carbohydrates can cause our blood sugar levels to spike, which can lead to fatigue, cravings, and even weight gain. Understanding carbohydrates and the glycemic index can help us make informed food choices and lead a healthier lifestyle. By focusing on complex carbohydrates with a low GI, we can ensure that we are providing our bodies with the energy they need to function properly. Eating a balanced diet that is rich in fiber, low in simple carbohydrates, and low in sugar can help us maintain a healthy weight and regulate our blood sugar levels.

Chapter 2

Asian Cooking Basics

Asian cooking is a style of cuisine that has been enjoyed around the world for centuries. It is characterized by its use of spices, aromatic flavors, and unique ingredients. While there is a wide variety of dishes and techniques used in Asian cooking, there are some basics that are common to all styles. The first step in any Asian cooking is to create a flavorful base. Depending on the dish, this may involve sautéing vegetables or aromatics such as garlic, ginger, and onions in oil. This will provide a flavorful foundation for the dish. Next, the main ingredients will be added. This could include proteins such as chicken, beef, pork, or seafood, as well as vegetables, noodles, and rice.

The ingredients are then cooked until they are tender, usually over high heat. Once the ingredients are cooked, it's time to add the seasonings. This is where Asian cooking really shines. Spices such as chili peppers, star anise, and turmeric are used to add flavor and depth. Soy sauce and fish sauce are also commonly used for added umami. Finally, the dish is finished with a variety of garnishes and condiments. These can range from herbs such as cilantro and basil to pickled vegetables, peanuts, and sesame seeds. Once you get the basics of Asian cooking down, you can begin experimenting with different ingredients and flavor combinations. With a few simple ingredients and some imagination, you can create delicious and flavorful dishes that will wow your family and friends.

Whether you're a beginner or a seasoned cook, Asian cooking is a great way to explore the flavors of the East. By following these basic principles and exploring the different ingredients and techniques, you can create an amazing array of dishes that will tantalize your taste buds.

Utensils and Equipment used in Asian Cooking

Asian cuisine is an incredibly diverse range of cooking styles and flavors. It encompasses many countries, including Japan, China, India, Thailand, and more. Each culture has its own unique culinary traditions and ingredients, but there are some common utensils and equipment used in Asian cooking. Knowing and understanding these tools can help you create delicious, authentic dishes. One of the most commonly used pieces of equipment in Asian cooking is the wok. It's a large, round-bottomed pan that's used for stir-frying, steaming, and deep-frying. It's perfect for quickly cooking food over high heat, and it's essential for achieving the signature smoky flavor of many Asian dishes.

In addition, a wok can also be used to braise and simmer dishes. Another important piece of equipment used in Asian cooking is the cleaver. It's a large, sharp knife that's perfect for slicing, dicing, and mincing a variety of ingredients. It's usually made of stainless steel and has a heavy, rectangular blade. Cleavers are great for preparing a wide range of dishes, from soups and stews to stir-fries and curries. Rice cookers are also popular pieces of equipment in many Asian kitchens. These small appliances are designed to perfectly cook rice in a short amount of time. They can also be used to steam vegetables and other dishes. Rice cookers come in various sizes and styles, ranging from simple models to more advanced ones with multiple functions. In addition to the above, there are other utensils used in Asian cooking that are worth mentioning. The mortar and pestle is a great tool for crushing and grinding spices and herbs. It's also great for making pastes and sauces. A rolling pin is perfect for rolling out thin dough for noodles and dumplings. And a pair of chopsticks is essential for eating many Asian dishes. These are just some of the utensils and equipment used in Asian cooking. Knowing and understanding these tools can help you create delicious, authentic dishes. With a few simple pieces of equipment, you'll be able to create a wide range of Asian dishes. So next time you're in the kitchen, make sure to have these essential tools on hand.

Techniques, Tools and Ingredients of Asian Cooking

Asian cuisine is a diverse and unique culinary art form that has been around for centuries. It is characterized by its unique use of ingredients, techniques, and tools, which are essential for creating authentic Asian dishes. When it comes to ingredients, Asian cooking utilizes a wide variety of vegetables, meats, and spices that are both familiar and exotic. Common vegetables used in Asian cooking include bok choy, garlic, ginger, water chestnuts, bamboo shoots, and shiitake mushrooms. Common meats include pork, beef, chicken, duck, and seafood such as shrimp, squid, and fish. Some of the more popular spices used in Asian cooking are soy sauce, oyster sauce, fish sauce, and sesame oil.

Techniques are an essential part of Asian cooking. Stir-frying, steaming, and deep-frying are all common methods used to prepare Asian dishes. Stir-frying is a technique where ingredients are quickly cooked in a hot pan with oil. This method helps to retain the flavors and preserve the texture of the ingredients. Steaming is another popular technique used in Asian cooking, where ingredients are cooked in a closed container with a small amount of liquid. This helps to preserve the flavors and nutrients of the ingredients. Deep-frying is a method of cooking where food is submerged in hot oil, resulting in a crispy exterior and a flavorful interior. In addition to techniques, tools are also a key part of Asian cooking. Common tools used in Asian cooking include woks, bamboo steamers, and cleavers.

Woks are a large, round-bottomed pan that is used for stir-frying, deep-frying, and steaming. Bamboo steamers are cylindrical baskets used to steam small pieces of food. Lastly, cleavers are large knives used for cutting, slicing, and dicing. Asian cuisine is a complex and flavorful culinary art form that requires the skillful use of techniques, tools, and ingredients. By mastering these techniques, tools, and ingredients, one can create authentic and delicious Asian dishes. With the right equipment and ingredients, anyone can become an expert in Asian cooking!

Popular Asian Herbs and Spices

Popular Asian herbs and spices have been used for centuries to create diverse, flavorful and healthy dishes from all corners of the world. From the spiciness of Indian curries to the subtle sweetness of Chinese stir-fries, each culture has its own unique way of using herbs and spices to bring out the best in their cuisine. In this essay, we will explore some of the most popular Asian herbs and spices and discuss how they can be used to add flavor and nutrition to your dishes. One of the most popular Asian herbs is cilantro, otherwise known as coriander. Cilantro is a leafy green herb that has a unique citrusy and nutty flavor, and it is often used in salads and as a garnish. It is also sometimes used in Southeast Asian cuisine as a flavorful addition to curries, soups, and sauces. Cilantro is high in Vitamin A, Vitamin C, and Vitamin K, making it a nutritious addition to your dishes. Another popular Asian spice is turmeric, a yellow-orange spice that is commonly used in Indian cuisine. Turmeric is known for its anti-inflammatory properties and its ability to help reduce pain, swelling, and inflammation. It has a slightly bitter flavor that can be used to add depth and complexity to dishes such as curries and stews.

Turmeric is also a good source of antioxidants, making it a great addition to your diet. Ginger is another popular Asian herb and spice that has many culinary and medicinal uses. It has a pungent, spicy flavor and can be used in a variety of dishes to add flavor and nutrition. Ginger is often used in stir-fries, soups, curries, and teas, and it is also known to have anti-inflammatory and anti-nausea properties. In addition, ginger is a good source of manganese, magnesium, and Vitamin B6, making it a great addition to your diet. Garlic is another popular Asian herb and spice that has a strong, pungent flavor. It is often used in stir-fries, curries, and sauces, and it can also be used to season meats, fish, and vegetables. Garlic is a good source of manganese, Vitamin B6, and Vitamin C, and it is also known to have anti-inflammatory and antioxidant properties.

Finally, chili peppers are another popular Asian spice that can be used to add heat and flavor to dishes. Chili peppers are known for their spicy flavor and can be used to make spicy curries, sauces, and stews. They are a good source of Vitamin C and iron, and they are also known to have anti-inflammatory and antioxidant properties. In conclusion, popular Asian herbs and spices can be used to add flavor and nutrition to your dishes. From cilantro to garlic, each herb and spice has its own unique flavor and health benefits, and they can be used to create a variety of flavorful and nutritious dishes. So, if you're looking for a way to add flavor and nutrition to your meals, consider adding some of these popular Asian herbs and spices to your dishes.

Chapter 3

Recipes

Asian recipes for diabetics focus on using ingredients that are low in sugar, fat, and sodium, such as fresh vegetables, lean meats, fish, and grains. Many recipes can be made low-carb and low-calorie by substituting vegetables for starches, such as using bell peppers instead of noodles. Ingredients like garlic, ginger, and cinnamon can also be used to add flavor without adding sugar. Common cooking techniques used in Asian recipes for diabetics include stir-frying and steaming, as they are healthier ways to cook food than deep-frying. In addition to being low in sugar and fat, Asian recipes for diabetics should be packed with fiber-rich ingredients such as beans, legumes, and whole grains.

Fiber helps to minimize the impact of carbohydrates on blood sugar levels. Diabetics should also make sure to include lean protein sources in their meals, such as eggs, tofu, and fish. Asian food is often known for its spiciness, but diabetics should be cautious when using spices. Spices like chili, cayenne, and garlic can add flavor without adding extra sugar or sodium. However, some spices do contain sugar, like curry powder, so it's important to read labels carefully. Finally, Asian recipes for diabetics can be made even healthier by incorporating superfoods. Superfoods are nutrient-rich foods that are packed with vitamins, minerals, and antioxidants.

Examples include green tea, which is full of antioxidants that can help reduce inflammation and stabilize blood sugar levels; and mushrooms, which are low in carbs and contain essential vitamins and minerals that can help keep blood sugar levels stable. By incorporating these healthy ingredients and cooking techniques, Asian recipes for diabetics can be flavorful, nutritious, and diabetes friendly.

Soups

Diabetic-friendly Asian soups are soups that are made with ingredients that are low in calories and carbohydrates, and provide a variety of health benefits. These soups typically contain vegetables, herbs, and spices that are known to help regulate blood sugar, improve digestion, and boost the immune system. Additionally, these soups are often low in sodium and fat, making them an ideal addition to any diabetic diet.

Vegetable Miso Soup

Ingredients

- 2 tablespoons miso paste

- 4 cups vegetable broth

- 2 teaspoons grated ginger

- 1 garlic clove, minced

- 2 cups sliced mushrooms

- 2 cups julienned carrots

- 2 cups chopped kale

- 2 tablespoons low sodium soy sauce

- 2 teaspoons sesame oil

Instructions

1. In a large pot, heat the miso paste and vegetable broth over medium-high heat until it begins to simmer.

2. Reduce the heat to low and add the ginger, garlic, mushrooms, carrots, and kale. Simmer for 10 minutes.

3. Stir in the soy sauce and sesame oil and cook for an additional 5 minutes.

4. Serve hot.

Nutritional Value

Calories: 126

Fat: 5.5 g

Carbohydrates: 13 g

Protein: 6.5 g

Egg Drop Soup

Prep Time: 10 minutes

Cook Time: 10 minutes

Total Time: 20 minutes

Servings: 4

Nutritional Value

Calories: 91 kcal

Carbohydrates: 5 g

Protein: 5 g

Fat: 4 g

Sodium: 762 mg

Ingredients

- 4 cups low-sodium chicken broth
- 2 tablespoons low-sodium soy sauce
- 2 tablespoons cornstarch
- 1/4 teaspoon ground ginger
- 2 large eggs

• 2 tablespoons chopped scallions

Instructions

1. In a large pot, combine chicken broth, soy sauce, cornstarch, and ground ginger. Bring to a boil over medium-high heat.

2. In a small bowl, whisk together the eggs and scallions.

3. Slowly pour the egg mixture into the boiling broth, stirring constantly.

4. Reduce the heat to low and cook for 5 minutes, stirring occasionally.

5. Remove from heat and serve.

Hot and Sour Soup

Prep time: 15 minutes

Cook time: 25 minutes

Total time: 40 minutes

Ingredients

-1 tablespoon olive oil

-1 cup sliced mushrooms

-1 cup diced carrots

-1/2 cup diced onions

-2 cloves garlic, minced

-2 tablespoons fresh ginger, grated

-1 teaspoon red pepper flakes

-4 cups low-sodium vegetable broth

-1/4 cup low-sodium soy sauce

-2 tablespoons red wine vinegar

-2 tablespoons cornstarch

-2 tablespoons water

-1/2 cup firm tofu, diced

-1/2 teaspoon black pepper

-1/4 cup sliced green onions

Instructions

1. Heat olive oil in a large pot over medium-high heat.

2. Add mushrooms, carrots, onions, garlic, ginger, and red pepper flakes. Cook for 5 minutes, stirring occasionally.

3. Add vegetable broth, soy sauce, and red wine vinegar. Bring to a simmer.

4. In a small bowl, whisk together the cornstarch and water until completely combined.

5. Slowly pour the cornstarch mixture into the soup, stirring constantly until the soup has thickened.

6. Add the tofu and black pepper. Simmer for 10 minutes.

7. Add the green onions and simmer for an additional 5 minutes.

8. Serve hot.

Nutrition Value (per serving)

Calories: 140

Fat: 5g

Carbohydrates: 12g

Protein: 7g

Sodium: 1040mg

Chicken and Rice Soup

Prep Time: 10 minutes

Cook Time: 25 minutes

Total Time: 35 minutes

Servings: 4

Ingredients

- 2 tablespoons olive oil

- 1 large onion, diced

- 2 cloves garlic, chopped

- 2 teaspoons ground ginger

- 2 tablespoons low-sodium soy sauce

- 1 teaspoon sesame oil

- 8 cups low-sodium chicken broth

- 2 large boneless, skinless chicken breasts, diced

- 2 cups cooked brown or white rice

- 2 carrots, thinly sliced

- 2 celery stalks, thinly sliced

- 1/2 cup frozen peas

- 2 tablespoons chopped fresh cilantro

Instructions

1. Heat the olive oil in a large pot over medium heat. Add the onion and garlic and sauté until the onion is translucent, about 3 minutes.

2. Add the ginger, soy sauce, and sesame oil and stir to combine.

3. Add the chicken broth, chicken, and rice and bring to a boil. Reduce the heat to low and simmer for 15 minutes.

4. Add the carrots, celery, and peas and simmer for an additional 5 minutes.

5. Remove from heat and stir in the cilantro.

Nutritional Value Per Serving (1/4 of recipe)

Calories: 341

Fat: 9 g

Carbohydrates: 33 g

Protein: 29 g

Sodium: 665 mg

Fiber: 4 g

Vegetable Soup

Total Time: 50 minutes

Servings: 6

Ingredients

-2 tablespoons of vegetable oil

-1 teaspoon of grated ginger

-1 teaspoon of minced garlic

-2 cups of diced carrots

-2 cups of diced celery

-2 cups of diced zucchini

-1 cup of diced red bell pepper

-4 cups of low-sodium vegetable broth

-2 tablespoons of soy sauce

-1 teaspoon of sesame oil

-1 teaspoon of crushed red pepper flakes

-1/2 teaspoon of sugar

-1/2 teaspoon of black pepper

-3 cups of cooked brown rice

-2 cups of cooked edamame

-1/4 cup of chopped scallions

Instructions

1. Heat the vegetable oil in a large pot over medium heat.

2. Add the ginger and garlic and cook for 1 minute.

3. Add the carrots, celery, zucchini, and bell pepper and cook for 5 minutes.

4. Add the vegetable broth, soy sauce, sesame oil, red pepper flakes, sugar, and black pepper.

5. Bring to a boil, then reduce the heat and simmer for 15 minutes.

6. Add the cooked rice and edamame and simmer for 10 minutes.

7. Add the scallions and cook for 5 minutes.

8. Serve hot.

Nutritional Value

Calories: 203

Fat: 7 g

Carbohydrates: 28 g

Protein: 7 g

Fiber: 4 g

Sugar: 5 g

Clear Mushroom Soup

Time Required: 30 minutes

Nutritional Value

Calories: 117

Carbohydrates: 11 g

Fiber: 1 g

Protein: 4 g

Ingredients

- 2 tablespoons olive oil

- 1/2 cup diced onion

- 2 cloves garlic, minced

- 2 cups sliced mushrooms

- 1 teaspoon fresh grated ginger

- 1 teaspoon low sodium soy sauce

- 2 cups low sodium chicken broth

- 1/4 teaspoon freshly ground white pepper

- 1/4 cup fresh cilantro, chopped

- 2 tablespoons fresh basil, chopped

Instructions

1. Heat the oil in a large saucepan over medium heat.

2. Add the onion and garlic and sauté for 3 minutes.

3. Add the mushrooms and fry for another 3 minutes.

4. Add the ginger, soy sauce, chicken broth, and white pepper. Bring to a boil and then reduce the heat to a simmer.

5. Simmer for 15 minutes.

6. Add the cilantro and basil and stir to combine.

7. Serve hot. Enjoy!

Bamboo Shoot Soup

Ingredients

- 1 tablespoon vegetable oil

- 1/2 cup diced onion

- 2 cloves garlic, minced

- 1 teaspoon fresh ginger, minced

- 2 cups vegetable broth

- 1 cup bamboo shoots, sliced

- 2 tablespoons low sodium soy sauce

- 1 teaspoon sesame oil

- 2 tablespoons cornstarch

- 1/4 cup water

- 1/4 cup chopped fresh cilantro

Instructions

1. Heat oil in a large saucepan over medium heat.

2. Add onion, garlic, and ginger and cook for 3-4 minutes, until softened.

3. Add broth, bamboo shoots, soy sauce, and sesame oil and bring to a boil.

4. Reduce heat and simmer for 15 minutes.

5. In a small bowl, whisk together cornstarch and water until combined.

6. Slowly stir into the soup and simmer for an additional 5 minutes, until thickened.

7. Remove from heat and stir in fresh cilantro.

Nutritional Value

Calories: 96

Fat: 6g

Carbohydrates: 8g

Protein: 3g

Fiber: 1g

Sodium: 633mg

Vegetable Broth Soup

Time Required: 40 minutes

Servings: 2

Nutritional Value

Calories: 116

Carbs: 20 g

Protein: 6 g

Fat: 2 g

Ingredients

- 2 cups of vegetable broth

- 2 tablespoons of low sodium soy sauce

- 1 teaspoon of sesame oil

- 1 teaspoon of fresh grated ginger

- 1 garlic clove, minced

- ½ cup of sliced mushrooms

- ½ cup of diced carrots

- ½ cup of finely chopped broccoli

- ½ cup of diced bell peppers

- 2 green onions, sliced

- 2 teaspoons of cornstarch

Instructions

1. In a large pot, heat the vegetable broth and soy sauce over medium heat.

2. Once it comes to a gentle boil, add in the sesame oil, ginger, garlic, mushrooms, carrots, broccoli, bell peppers and green onions.

3. Reduce the heat to low and simmer for 25 minutes.

4. In a small bowl, mix together the cornstarch and 1 tablespoon of cold water.

5. Slowly stir the cornstarch mixture into the soup, stirring constantly until it thickens.

6. Simmer for an additional 10 minutes.

7. Serve the soup hot and enjoy!

Tofu and Vegetable Soup

Prep Time: 10 minutes

Cook Time: 15 minutes

Total Time: 25 minutes

Ingredients

- 2 tablespoons olive oil

- 1 onion, diced

- 2 cloves garlic, minced

- 2 carrots, diced

- 2 stalks celery, diced

- 4 cups vegetable stock

- 2 cups diced potatoes

- 1 cup diced tofu

- 1 cup frozen peas

- 1 teaspoon dried thyme

- ½ teaspoon dried oregano

- Salt and pepper, to taste

Instructions

1. Heat the olive oil in a large pot over medium-high heat.

2. Add the onion, garlic, carrots, and celery and cook until softened, about 5 minutes.

3. Add the vegetable stock, potatoes, tofu, peas, thyme, oregano, and salt and pepper. Bring to a boil.

4. Reduce the heat to medium-low and simmer until the potatoes are tender, about 10 minutes.

5. Serve hot.

Nutritional Value (Per Serving)

Calories: 211

Fat: 8.3g

Carbohydrates: 22.5g

Protein: 10.5g

Coconut Milk Soup

Time Required: 25 minutes

Servings: 4

Ingredients

- 1 tablespoon olive oil
- 2 cloves garlic, minced
- 1 onion, chopped
- 2 tablespoons fresh ginger, minced
- 2 tablespoons red curry paste
- 2 cans light coconut milk
- 2 cups vegetable broth
- 1 cup carrots, diced
- 1 cup celery, diced
- 1 cup red bell pepper, diced
- 2 tablespoons lime juice
- Salt and pepper to taste

Instructions

1. Heat olive oil in a large pot at medium heat. Add garlic, onion, and ginger and fry for 3 minutes.

2. Stir in curry paste and cook for another 2 minutes.

3. Add coconut milk, vegetable broth, carrots, celery, and red bell pepper. Bring to a boil, reduce heat to low, cover, and simmer for 15 minutes or until vegetables are tender.

4. Remove from heat and stir in lime juice.

5. Season with salt and pepper.

Nutritional Value (per serving)

Calories: 206

Fat: 14.4g

Carbohydrates: 18.2g

Protein: 4.7g

Sodium: 613mg

Fiber: 4.2g

Spinach and Tofu Soup

Prep Time: 10 minutes

Cook Time: 20 minutes

Total Time: 30 minutes

Servings: 4

Nutritional Value

Calories: 127 kcal

Carbohydrates: 10.7g

Protein: 8.1g

Fat: 7.2g

Ingredients

* 2 tablespoons olive oil

* 1 onion, diced

* 2 cloves garlic, minced

* 2 cups vegetable broth

* 2 cups water

* 2 cups baby spinach

* 1 teaspoon dried oregano

* 1/2 teaspoon dried thyme

* 1/4 teaspoon black pepper

* 1 (14-ounce) package extra-firm tofu, drained and cubed

* Salt and pepper, to taste

Instructions

1. Heat the olive oil in a large pot over medium heat.

2. Add the onion and garlic and cook until softened, about 5 minutes.

3. Add the vegetable broth, water, spinach, oregano, thyme, and black pepper and bring to a boil.

4. Add the tofu and cook for 10 minutes.

5. Season with salt and pepper, to taste.

6. Serve hot. Enjoy!

Chinese Celery Soup

Servings: 2

Prep Time: 10 minutes

Cook Time: 20 minutes

Nutritional Value

Calories: 189

Protein: 10.1g

Fat: 6.8g

Carbs: 23.1g

Ingredients

-2 tablespoons olive oil

-1 onion, diced

-4 cloves garlic, minced

-2 stalks celery, diced

-1/4 teaspoon ground black pepper

-4 cups vegetable broth

-1/2 cup uncooked quinoa

-1/4 cup chopped fresh parsley

Instructions

1. Heat oil in a large saucepan over medium heat.

2. Add onion and garlic and cook until softened, about 5 minutes.

3. Add celery and black pepper and cook until celery is tender, about 5 minutes.

4. Add vegetable broth, quinoa, and parsley. Bring to a boil, reduce heat to low, and simmer for 10 minutes.

5. Serve soup hot. Enjoy!

Burdock Root Soup

Prep Time: 10 minutes

Cook Time: 25 minutes

Total Time: 35 minutes

Ingredients

- 2 tablespoons olive oil

- 1 onion, diced

- 2 cloves garlic, minced

- 1 pound burdock root, peeled and diced

- 4 cups vegetable broth

- 1 teaspoon dried thyme

- ½ teaspoon sea salt

- 2 tablespoons fresh parsley, chopped

Instructions

1. Heat olive oil in a large pot at medium-high heat.

2. Add onion and garlic and sauté for 3 minutes.

3. Add burdock root and sauté for an additional 2 minutes.

4. Add vegetable broth, thyme, and sea salt.

5. Bring to a boil, reduce heat, and simmer for 20 minutes or until the burdock root is tender.

6. Remove from heat and stir in parsley.

7. Serve warm.

Nutritional Value (per serving)

Calories: 109

Fat: 6.2g

Carbohydrates: 13.2g

Protein: 2.7g

Fiber: 3.4g

Broccoli and Mushroom Soup

Servings: 4

Prep Time: 10 minutes

Cook Time: 30 minutes

Total Time: 40 minutes

Ingredients

* 4 cups broccoli florets

* 1 cup chopped mushrooms

* 2 cloves garlic, minced

* 1 teaspoon olive oil

* 2 cups low-sodium vegetable broth

* 1/4 teaspoon dried thyme

* 1/4 teaspoon dried oregano

* Salt and pepper to taste

Instructions

1. Heat the olive oil in a large pot over medium heat.

2. Add the garlic and mushrooms, and cook for 3-4 minutes, stirring occasionally.

3. Add the broccoli, vegetable broth, thyme and oregano.

4. Bring the mixture to a boil, then reduce the heat and simmer for 20-25 minutes, until the broccoli is tender.

5. Season with salt and pepper to taste.

6. Serve hot.

Nutritional Value

Calories: 65 kcal

Carbohydrates: 8.2 g

Protein: 3.8 g

Fat: 2.6 g

Saturated Fat: 0.4 g

Cholesterol: 0 mg

Sodium: 209 mg

Fiber: 2.6 g

Sugar: 2.2 g

Japanese Pumpkin Soup

Time Required: 30 minutes

Servings: 4

Nutritional Value:

Calories: 157 per serving

Carbs: 13.6g

Fat: 7.2g

Protein: 10.5g

Ingredients

1 tablespoon olive oil

1 medium onion, chopped

2 cloves garlic, minced

2 teaspoons grated fresh ginger

3 cups chicken or vegetable broth

2 cups cubed fresh pumpkin (or canned pumpkin)

1 teaspoon Chinese 5-spice powder

2 tablespoons low-sodium soy sauce

1 teaspoon honey

1/4 cup plain Greek yogurt

1/4 cup chopped cilantro

Instructions

1. Heat olive oil in a large saucepan over medium heat.

2. Add onion and garlic and cook, stirring, until softened, about 5 minutes.

3. Add ginger, broth, pumpkin and Chinese 5-spice powder, and bring to a boil.

4. Reduce heat and simmer, covered, until pumpkin is tender, about 15 minutes.

5. Remove from heat and, using an immersion blender, puree soup until smooth.

6. Stir in soy sauce and honey.

7. Ladle soup into bowls and top with a dollop of Greek yogurt and a sprinkle of cilantro. Enjoy!

Seaweed Soup

Time Required: 15 minutes

Servings: 2

Nutritional Value (per serving)

Calories: 74

Fat: 0.4g

Carbohydrates: 9.7g

Protein: 4.7g

Ingredients

- 2 cups of vegetable broth

- 2 teaspoons of low sodium soy sauce

- 2 teaspoons of sesame oil

- 2 teaspoons of fresh grated ginger

- 2 cloves of garlic, minced

- 2 tablespoons of dried seaweed

- 2 tablespoons of chopped scallions

Instructions

1. In a medium saucepan, bring the vegetable broth to a boil.

2. Add the soy sauce, sesame oil, ginger, and garlic.

3. Reduce the heat to low and simmer for 10 minutes.

4. Add the seaweed and simmer for an additional 5 minutes.

5. Remove from heat and stir in the scallions.

6. Serve hot. Enjoy!

Chinese Cabbage Soup

Time Required: 25 minutes

Ingredients

- 1 tablespoon olive oil

- 1 onion, chopped

- 2 cloves garlic, minced

- 1 teaspoon ground ginger

- 2 cups vegetable broth

- 1/2 cup water

- 1 head Chinese cabbage, chopped

- 2 carrots, peeled and diced

- 1/4 teaspoon black pepper

- 2 tablespoons low-sodium soy sauce

Instructions

1. Heat the oil in a large pot over medium heat.

2. Add the onion and sauté for 5 minutes, stirring occasionally.

3. Add the garlic and ginger and cook for an additional minute.

4. Pour in the broth and water. Add the cabbage, carrots, pepper, and soy sauce.

5. Bring to a boil and reduce the heat to low. Simmer for 20 minutes.

6. Serve hot.

Nutritional Value

Calories: 63

Fat: 2.7g

Carbohydrates: 8.4g

Protein: 2.4g

Sodium: 595mg

Winter Melon Soup

Total Time: 30 minutes

Servings: 4

Ingredients:

- 2 tablespoons vegetable oil
- 1 teaspoon minced garlic
- 1 teaspoon minced ginger
- 2 cups diced winter melon
- 4 cups chicken broth
- 1 teaspoon salt
- 1 tablespoon light soy sauce

- 2 tablespoons chopped cilantro

Instructions

1. Heat the oil in a large pot over medium heat.

2. Add the garlic and ginger, and cook for 1 minute.

3. Add the winter melon, chicken broth, salt and soy sauce. Bring to a boil, reduce the heat and simmer for 15 minutes.

4. Remove from the heat and stir in the cilantro.

5. Serve hot.

Nutritional Value

Calories: 97

Total Fat: 6.3g

Saturated Fat: 0.7g

Cholesterol: 0mg

Sodium: 793mg

Total Carbohydrate: 7.4g

Dietary Fiber: 1.3g

Sugars: 5.3g

Protein: 2.5g

Sweet Corn Soup

Time Required: 20 minutes

Ingredients

- 2 cups of frozen sweet corn
- 1 cup of low-sodium vegetable broth
- 1 cup of skim milk
- 1 teaspoon of olive oil
- Salt and pepper to taste

Instructions

1. Heat the olive oil in a medium-sized saucepan over medium-high heat.
2. Add the frozen corn and sauté for 5 minutes.
3. Add the vegetable broth and bring to a boil.
4. Reduce the heat to low and simmer for 10 minutes.
5. Add the skim milk and stir to combine.
6. Simmer for an additional 5 minutes.
7. Season with salt and pepper to taste.
8. Serve warm.

Nutritional Value

Calories: 120

Fat: 4.3g

Carbs: 18.3g

Protein: 4.6g

Carrot Soup

Time Required: 30 minutes

Ingredients

- 2 tablespoons olive oil

- 1 onion, diced

- 4 cloves garlic, minced

- 1 teaspoon ground cumin

- 6 cups vegetable broth

- 2 cups peeled and diced carrots

- 1/2 teaspoon dried thyme

- 1/4 teaspoon ground nutmeg

- Salt and pepper, to taste

Instructions

1. Heat the oil in a large pot over medium heat.

2. Add the onion and garlic and cook until softened, about 5 minutes.

3. Add the cumin and cook for another minute.

4. Pour in the broth and bring to a boil.

5. Add the carrots, thyme, and nutmeg and season with salt and pepper.

6. Reduce the heat to low and simmer until the carrots are tender, about 20 minutes.

7. Use an immersion blender to puree the soup until smooth.

8. Serve warm.

Nutritional Value

- Calories: 152

- Total Fat: 7g

- Sodium: 638mg

- Total Carbohydrates: 17g

- Protein: 4g

- Vitamin A: 220% DV

- Vitamin C: 12% DV

Bok Choy Soup

Prep Time: 10 minutes

Cook Time: 25 minutes

Total Time: 35 minutes

Ingredients

- 2 tablespoons olive oil

- 1 small onion, diced

- 1 tablespoon minced garlic

- 2 tablespoons fresh ginger, peeled and chopped

- 2 cups vegetable broth

- 1/2 teaspoon sesame oil

- 2 cups Bok Choy, roughly chopped

- 2 tablespoons low sodium soy sauce

- 2 tablespoons brown sugar

- 2 tablespoons rice vinegar

- 1/4 teaspoon ground black pepper

Instructions

1. Heat olive oil in a large pot over medium heat.

2. Add onion and garlic, and cook until softened, about 5 minutes.

3. Add ginger and cook for 1 minute.

4. Pour in the vegetable broth, sesame oil, Bok Choy, soy sauce, brown sugar, rice vinegar, and black pepper.

5. Bring to a boil and then reduce heat to low and simmer for 20 minutes.

6. Serve warm.

Nutritional Value

Calories: 150

Total Fat: 7g

Saturated Fat: 1g

Cholesterol: 0mg

Sodium: 590mg

Total Carbohydrates: 18g

Dietary Fiber: 3g

Sugars: 9g

Protein: 3g

Chinese Spinach Soup

Time Required: 15 minutes

Servings: 2

Nutritional Value

Calories: 64

Fat: 1g

Carbohydrates: 11.5g

Protein: 4.5g

Ingredients

- 2 cups of low-sodium vegetable broth
- 1/2 cup diced onion
- 1/2 teaspoon of minced garlic
- 2 cups of fresh baby spinach
- 2 tablespoons of low-sodium soy sauce
- 1 teaspoon of sesame oil
- 1/2 teaspoon of ground ginger
- 1/4 teaspoon of chili flakes

- 1/4 teaspoon of black pepper

Instructions

1. Heat a medium pot over medium-high heat.

2. Add the vegetable broth, onion, and garlic and bring to a boil.

3. Reduce the heat to low and simmer for 10 minutes.

4. Add in the spinach and continue to simmer for another 5 minutes.

5. Add the soy sauce, sesame oil, ginger, chili flakes, and black pepper and stir to combine.

6. Simmer for another 5 minutes or until the spinach is cooked through.

7. Serve and enjoy!

Tom Yum Soup

Time Required: 20 minutes

Ingredients

- 1 cup low-sodium vegetable broth

- 2 tablespoons fish sauce

- 2 tablespoons freshly squeezed lime juice

- 2 cloves garlic, minced
- 2 tablespoons grated ginger
- 1 teaspoon chili paste
- 1 cup sliced mushrooms
- 2 tablespoons chopped scallions
- 1/2 cup chopped tomatoes
- 4 ounces cooked shrimp

Instructions

1. In a medium saucepan, combine the vegetable broth, fish sauce, lime juice, garlic, ginger and chili paste. Bring to a boil over medium-high heat.

2. Add the mushrooms, scallions and tomatoes. Simmer for 5 minutes.

3. Add the cooked shrimp and simmer for an additional 5 minutes.

4. Serve hot. Enjoy!

Nutritional Value

Calories: 148 kcal

Fat: 4.6 g

Carbs: 14.7 g

Protein: 7.5 g

Hot and Sour Fish Soup

Prep Time: 10 minutes

Cook Time: 20 minutes

Total Time: 30 minutes

Servings: 4

Nutritional Value

Calories: 146

Carbohydrates: 10.3g

Protein: 9.3g

Fat: 8.3g

Ingredients

1 tablespoon olive oil

2 cloves garlic, minced

1 teaspoon grated ginger

1 red bell pepper, diced

1 carrot, diced

1/2 cup mushrooms, sliced

4 cups low-sodium vegetable broth

2 tablespoons low-sodium soy sauce

1/4 teaspoon ground black pepper

1/4 teaspoon red pepper flakes

1 tablespoon cornstarch

1 tablespoon cold water

1/4 cup light coconut milk

8 ounces white fish, such as tilapia or cod, cut into 1-inch cubes

1/4 cup cilantro, chopped

Instructions

1. Heat the olive oil in a large pot at medium heat. Add the garlic and ginger, and stir for 1 minute.

2. Add the bell pepper, carrot, and mushrooms, and cook for 3 minutes.

3. Add the vegetable broth, soy sauce, ground black pepper, and red pepper flakes, and bring to a boil.

4. Reduce the heat and simmer for 15 minutes.

5. In a small bowl, whisk together the cornstarch and cold water. Slowly add the cornstarch mixture to the soup, stirring constantly.

6. Add the coconut milk and fish, and heat for an additional 5 minutes.

7. Remove from heat and stir in the cilantro.

8. Serve hot. Enjoy!

Tomato Soup

Time Required: 25 minutes

Ingredients

-2 tablespoons olive oil

-1 yellow onion, diced

-3 cloves garlic, minced

-2 cans of fire-roasted diced tomatoes

-4 cups low-sodium vegetable broth

-2 tablespoons tomato paste

-1 teaspoon dried oregano

-1 teaspoon dried basil

-1/2 teaspoon sea salt

-1/4 teaspoon freshly ground black pepper

-1/4 cup fresh basil leaves, chopped

Instructions

1. Heat the olive oil in a large saucepan over medium heat.

2. Add the onion and garlic and sauté for 5 minutes until the onion is softened.

3. Add the canned tomatoes, vegetable broth, tomato paste, oregano, dried basil, sea salt, and black pepper.

4. Bring the soup to a boil and then reduce the heat to low and simmer for 15 minutes.

5. Transfer to a blender and puree until smooth.

6. Return the soup to the saucepan and bring to a simmer.

7. Stir in the fresh basil leaves and serve.

Nutritional Value

Calories: 99 kcal

Carbohydrates: 11 g

Protein: 3 g

Fat: 5 g

Saturated Fat: 1 g

Sodium: 536 mg

Potassium: 408 mg

Fiber: 3 g

Sugar: 6 g

Vitamin A: 997 IU

Vitamin C: 28 mg

Calcium: 79 mg

Iron: 2 mg

Chicken Noodle Soup

Prep Time: 10 minutes

Cook Time: 40 minutes

Total Time: 50 minutes

Servings: 8

Nutrition Value (per serving)

Calories:172

Total Fat:3.3g

Saturated Fat: 0.8g

Monounsaturated Fat: 0.9g

Cholesterol:19mg

Sodium: 686mg

Carbohydrate:22.5g

Dietary Fiber:3.3g

Protein:12.3g

Ingredients

- 4 cups low-sodium chicken broth

- 2 cups water

- 2 stalks celery, diced

- 2 carrots, peeled and diced

- 1/2 onion, diced

- 1 teaspoon garlic powder

- 1 teaspoon dried thyme

- 1 bay leaf

- 2 chicken breasts, boneless and skinless, cut into cubes

- 1/2 teaspoon black pepper

- 1/2 teaspoon salt• 1/2 package of whole-wheat noodles (egg-free, if desired)

Instructions

1. In a large pot, add the chicken broth, water, celery, carrots, onion, garlic powder, thyme, and bay leaf. Bring to a boil.

2. Reduce the heat to low and add the chicken breasts. Simmer for 25 minutes.

3. Add the black pepper, salt, and noodles and simmer for another 10-15 minutes or until the noodles are cooked.

4. Serve the soup while hot. Enjoy!

Udon Noodle Soup

Time Required: 25 minutes

Ingredients

- 4 cups vegetable broth

- 2 cloves garlic, minced

- 2 tablespoons fresh ginger, grated

- 2 tablespoons reduced-sodium soy sauce

- 2 tablespoons rice vinegar

- 1 teaspoon sesame oil

- 1 teaspoon honey

- 8 oz. udon noodles

- 1 cup edamame
- 1 red bell pepper, sliced
- 1 cup shredded carrots
- 2 green onions, sliced

Instructions

1. In a large pot, bring the vegetable broth to a boil.

2. Add the garlic, ginger, soy sauce, rice vinegar, sesame oil, and honey. Stir to combine.

3. Add the udon noodles and cook for 8 minutes.

4. Add the edamame, bell pepper, carrots, and green onions. Cook for an additional 5 minutes.

5. Serve hot. Enjoy!

Nutritional Value

Calories: 459

Total Fat: 10g

Saturated Fat: 2g

Cholesterol: 19mg, Sodium: 1237mg

Total Carbohydrate: 72g

Dietary Fiber: 6g

Protein: 19g

Wakame Soup

Time Required: 15 minutes

Servings: 4

Ingredients

- 4 cups vegetable broth
- 1/2 cup dried wakame seaweed
- 1/2 cup sliced shiitake mushrooms
- 1/2 cup diced carrots
- 1/2 cup diced zucchini
- 2 tablespoons tamari
- 1 teaspoon grated ginger
- 1/4 teaspoon red pepper flakes

Instructions

1. Put the vegetable broth in a medium-sized pot and bring to a boil.

2. Add the wakame, mushrooms, carrots, zucchini, tamari, ginger, and red pepper flakes.

3. Simmer the soup for 10 minutes, stirring occasionally.

4. Serve the soup hot. Enjoy!

Nutritional Value

Calories: 92

Carbs: 12 g

Protein: 2 g

Fat: 4 g

Miso Eggplant Soup

Total Time: 25 minutes

Servings: 4

Ingredients

- 2 tablespoons canola oil

- 1 large onion, chopped

- 2 cloves garlic, minced

- 2 tablespoons minced fresh ginger

- 1 large eggplant, chopped

- 8 cups vegetable stock

- 2 tablespoons miso paste

- 2 tablespoons rice vinegar

- 2 tablespoons soy sauce

- 2 tablespoons sesame oil

- 1/2 teaspoon ground black pepper

- 2 tablespoons chopped fresh cilantro

Instructions

1. Heat canola oil in a large pot over medium-high heat. Add the onion, garlic, and ginger and cook until softened, about 3 minutes.

2. Add the eggplant and cook for 5 minutes, stirring occasionally.

3. Add the vegetable stock, miso paste, rice vinegar, soy sauce, sesame oil, and black pepper and bring to a boil.

4. Reduce heat to low and simmer for 10 minutes.

5. Stir in the cilantro and cook for 2 more minutes.

6. Serve hot.

Nutritional Value

Calories: 128 kcal

Fat: 7.4 g

Carbohydrates: 13.3 g

Protein: 3.3 g

Fiber: 3.2 g

Sugar: 6.7 g

Bok Choy and Tofu Soup

Time Required: 30 minutes

Ingredients

- 1 tablespoon vegetable oil

- 1/2 cup diced onion

- 2 cloves garlic, minced

- 2 cups vegetable broth

- 1 teaspoon fresh grated ginger

- 1/4 teaspoon red pepper flakes

- 1/4 teaspoon ground black pepper

- 1/4 teaspoon ground cumin

- 2 cups bok choy, chopped

- 1/2 cup firm tofu, cubed

- 1 tablespoon soy sauce

Instructions

1. Heat the oil in a large pot over medium heat.

2. Add the onion and garlic and cook until softened, about 5 minutes.

3. Add the vegetable broth, ginger, red pepper flakes, black pepper and cumin. Stir to combine.

4. Bring to a boil, then reduce heat and simmer for 10 minutes.

5. Add the bok choy and tofu, and cook for 5 minutes more.

6. Stir in the soy sauce and cook for 1 more minute.

7. Serve hot. Enjoy!

Nutritional Value:

Calories: 175

Carbs: 17 g

Fat: 7 g

Protein: 10 g

Side Dishes

Diabetes is a metabolic disorder that affects millions of people around the world. For those living with diabetes, it is important to make sure that the food they consume is both nutritious and diabetes-friendly. Fortunately, there is a wide range of Asian side dishes that can fit into a diabetes-friendly diet. One of the most popular diabetes-friendly side dishes in

Asian cuisine is steamed vegetables. Not only are steamed vegetables low in calories, but they are also packed with essential vitamins and minerals. Additionally, steamed vegetables have a lower glycemic index than boiled or fried vegetables, making them an ideal choice for those with diabetes. Examples of popular steamed vegetables in Asian cuisine include broccoli, cauliflower, carrots, mushrooms, and bok choy. Another great diabetes-friendly side dish is Asian-style salads. Salads are a great way to get a variety of nutrient-rich vegetables and fruits into your diet without adding a lot of calories. For an extra protein boost, try adding grilled chicken, tofu, or fish to your salad.

Popular Asian-style salads include seaweed salad, green papaya salad, and cucumber salad. Rice is another popular side dish in Asian cuisine. White rice can be high in carbohydrates and therefore not the best choice for those with diabetes. Fortunately, there are other types of rice that can fit into a diabetes-friendly diet. Brown rice, black rice, and wild rice are all lower in carbohydrates than white rice and provide a great source of fiber. Finally, Asian-style soups are an excellent diabetes-friendly side dish. Soups are low in calories and provide a great way to get a variety of vegetables into your diet. Popular soups in Asian cuisine include miso soup, chicken and corn soup, and hot and sour soup.

Overall, there are a wide range of Asian side dishes that can fit into a diabetes-friendly diet. From steamed vegetables and Asian-style salads to rice and soups, there is something for everyone. With a little bit of planning and creativity, those with diabetes can enjoy a variety of delicious and healthy Asian side dishes.

Stir-Fried Bok Choy with Garlic and Ginger

Total Time: 15 minutes

Servings: 4

Ingredients

- 2 tablespoons olive oil

- 4 cloves garlic, minced

- 2 teaspoons grated fresh ginger

- 2 heads of bok choy, washed and chopped

- 1 tablespoon low-sodium soy sauce

- 1 teaspoon sesame oil

- 2 teaspoons sesame seeds

Instructions

1. Heat the olive oil in a large skillet over medium-high heat.

2. Add the garlic and ginger and cook, stirring, for 1 minute.

3. Add the bok choy and cook, stirring occasionally, for 5 minutes.

4. Add the soy sauce, sesame oil, and sesame seeds and cook, stirring, for 3 minutes.

5. Serve hot.

Spicy Eggplant Stir-Fry

Prep Time: 10 minutes

Cook Time: 15 minutes

Total Time: 25 minutes

Servings: 4

Ingredients

- 1 large eggplant, cut into cubes

- 2 tablespoons olive oil

- 2 cloves garlic, minced

- 2 teaspoons chili powder

- 1 teaspoon ground cumin

- 1 teaspoon ground coriander

- 1/2 teaspoon sea salt

- 1/4 teaspoon black pepper

- 2 tablespoons chopped cilantro

Instructions

1. Heat oil in a large skillet over medium heat.

2. Add eggplant and stir-fry for about 5 minutes or until lightly browned.

3. Add garlic, chili powder, cumin, coriander, salt and pepper. Stir-fry for another 5 minutes or until eggplant is tender.

4. Remove from heat and stir in cilantro.

5. Serve hot.

Nutritional Value

Calories: 170

Fat: 11 g

Carbohydrates: 12 g

Protein: 3 g

Fiber: 4 g

Sugar: 5 g

Sodium: 222 mg

Cabbage and Tofu Stir-Fry

Total Time: 20 minutes

Servings: 4

Ingredients

- 2 tablespoons vegetable oil

- 1/2 teaspoon garlic, minced

- 1/2 teaspoon ginger, minced

- 1/2 head cabbage, shredded

- 8 ounces firm tofu, cut into cubes

- 2 tablespoons soy sauce

- 2 tablespoons sesame oil

Instructions

1. Heat vegetable oil in a large skillet over medium heat.

2. Add garlic and ginger and sauté until fragrant, about 1 minute.

3. Add cabbage and tofu and stir-fry until cabbage is tender, about 8 minutes.

4. Add soy sauce and sesame oil and stir-fry for an additional 1-2 minutes.

5. Serve hot.

Nutritional Value (per serving)

Calories: 197

Fat: 11.9g

Carbohydrates: 9.6g

Protein: 11.4g

Fiber: 3.2g

Sugar: 3.2g

Asian-Style Cauliflower Rice

Prep Time: 15 minutes

Cook Time: 5 minutes

Total Time: 20 minutes

Ingredients

- 1 head of cauliflower, cut into florets

- 1 tablespoon of coconut oil

- 2 cloves of garlic, minced

- 1 teaspoon of freshly grated ginger

- 2 tablespoons of low-sodium soy sauce

- 2 tablespoons of rice vinegar

- 1 teaspoon of sesame oil

- 1/2 teaspoon of red pepper flakes

- 1/4 cup of green onions, chopped

- Sesame seeds (optional)

Instructions

1. Place the cauliflower florets in a food processor and pulse until the cauliflower is the size of grains of rice.

2. Heat the coconut oil in a large pan over medium heat. Add the garlic and ginger and sauté for 1 minute.

3. Add the cauliflower to the pan and stir-fry for 2-3 minutes.

4. Add the soy sauce, rice vinegar, sesame oil, and red pepper flakes and stir to combine.

5. Cook for an additional 2 minutes or until the cauliflower is tender.

6. Remove from heat and stir in the green onions.

7. Serve hot, garnished with sesame seeds (optional).

Nutritional Value

Calories: 70

Total Fat: 3g

Sodium: 290mg

Total Carbohydrates: 8g

Dietary Fiber: 3g

Sugars: 3g

Protein: 3g

Rice Noodle and Vegetable Stir-Fry

Time Required: 20 minutes

Servings: 4

Ingredients

- 8 ounces rice noodles
- 1 tablespoon olive oil
- 2 cloves garlic, minced
- 1 onion, diced
- 2 carrots, sliced
- 1 bell pepper, sliced
- 1 cup snap peas
- 2 tablespoons low-sodium soy sauce
- 2 tablespoons rice vinegar
- 2 tablespoons sesame oil
- Sesame seeds, for garnish

Instructions

1. Cook the rice noodles according to package instructions. Drain and set aside.

2. Heat the olive oil in a large skillet or wok over medium heat. Add the garlic, onion, carrots, and bell pepper. Stir-fry for 5 minutes.

3. Add the snap peas and stir-fry for an additional 3 minutes.

4. Add the cooked noodles, soy sauce, rice vinegar, and sesame oil. Stir-fry for an additional 2 minutes.

5. Serve the stir-fry with sesame seeds for garnish. Enjoy!

Nutritional Value

Calories: 240

Carbohydrates: 33 g

Protein: 7 g

Fat: 8 g

Fiber: 4 g

Sodium: 270 mg

Cholesterol: 0 mg

Chinese-Style Baked Vegetables

Prep Time: 15 minutes

Cook Time: 30 minutes

Total Time: 45 minutes

Ingredients

- 1 cup broccoli florets

- 1 cup cauliflower florets

- 1 cup sliced mushrooms

- 1 cup julienne red bell pepper

- 1 cup julienne green bell pepper

- 1/4 cup olive oil

- 2 cloves garlic, minced

- 2 tablespoons low-sodium soy sauce

- 1 tablespoon sesame oil

- 1/2 teaspoon ground black pepper

Instructions

1. Oven should be preheated to 400 degrees Fahrenheit.

2. In a large bowl, combine broccoli, cauliflower, mushrooms, red and green bell peppers.

3. In a small bowl, whisk together olive oil, garlic, soy sauce, sesame oil and black pepper.

4. Pour the oil mixture over the vegetables and mix until all the vegetables are evenly coated.

5. Spread the vegetables in a single layer on a baking sheet.

6. Bake for 30 minutes, stirring once halfway through, until the vegetables are tender and lightly browned.

Nutritional Value (per serving)

Calories: 81

Fat: 6.3g

Carbohydrates: 5.7g

Fiber: 2.3g

Protein: 2.1g

Sugar: 2.2g

Sodium: 157mg

Low Carb Asian-Style Coleslaw

Ingredients

1/2 head cabbage, shredded

1/4 cup chopped green onions

1/4 cup sliced red bell pepper

1/4 cup matchstick carrots

2 tablespoons rice wine vinegar

1 tablespoon sesame oil

2 tablespoons low-sodium soy sauce

1 tablespoon sesame seeds

1 tablespoon honey

1/2 teaspoon grated fresh ginger

1/4 teaspoon garlic powder

Instructions

1. In a large bowl, combine the cabbage, green onion, red bell pepper, and carrots.

2. In a small bowl, whisk together the rice wine vinegar, sesame oil, soy sauce, sesame seeds, honey, ginger, garlic powder, salt, and pepper.

3. Pour the dressing over the coleslaw and toss to combine.

4. Refrigerate for at least 30 minutes before serving.

Nutritional Value

Calories: 118

Fat: 6.6g

Carbohydrate: 13.4g

Protein: 3.2g

Fiber: 3.5g

Sugar: 7.7g

Steamed Edamame with Soy Sauce

Prep Time: 5 minutes

Cook Time: 5 minutes

Total Time: 10 minutes

Servings: 4

Ingredients

- 2 cups fresh edamame, shelled
- 2 tablespoons low-sodium soy sauce
- 1 teaspoon sesame oil
- 1 teaspoon freshly grated ginger

Instructions

1. Boil a pot of water.
2. Add the edamame to the boiling water and cook for 5 minutes.

3. Drain the edamame and transfer to a bowl.

4. Add the soy sauce, sesame oil and ginger to the edamame and toss to combine.

5. Serve warm. Enjoy!

Nutritional Value

Calories: 105

Fat: 4.3g

Carbohydrates: 10.3g

Protein: 8.2g

Sodium: 552mg

Baked Asian-Style Eggplant

Time Required: 40 minutes

Servings: 4

Ingredients

- 2 large eggplants, cut into 1/2-inch thick slices

- 2 tablespoons olive oil

- 2 cloves garlic, minced

- 2 tablespoons reduced-sodium soy sauce

- 2 tablespoons rice vinegar

- 1 tablespoon sesame oil

- 1 tablespoon honey

- 2 teaspoons grated ginger

- 2 tablespoons chopped fresh cilantro

- 1/4 teaspoon red pepper flakes

Instructions

1. Preheat oven to 350°F.

2. Place eggplant slices on a baking sheet and brush with olive oil.

3. Bake for 20 minutes, flipping halfway through.

4. In a small bowl, whisk together garlic, soy sauce, rice vinegar, sesame oil, honey, ginger, cilantro, and red pepper flakes.

5. Once eggplant is finished baking, brush with the sauce and bake for an additional 20 minutes.

6. Serve hot. Enjoy!

Nutritional Value

Calories: 162

Fat: 8g

Carbohydrates: 17g

Protein: 3g

Fiber: 5g

Miso-Glazed Eggplant

Prep Time: 10 minutes

Cook Time: 30 minutes

Servings: 4

Ingredients

- 2 large eggplants, sliced into 1/2-inch thick rounds

- 1/4 cup white miso

- 2 tablespoons mirin

- 2 tablespoons rice vinegar

- 2 tablespoons toasted sesame oil

- 2 tablespoons honey

- 2 tablespoons freshly grated ginger

- 2 tablespoons garlic, minced

- 2 tablespoons sesame seeds

- 2 tablespoons vegetable oil

Instructions

1. Preheat the oven to 350°F.

2. In a small bowl, whisk together the miso, mirin, rice vinegar, sesame oil, honey, ginger, garlic, and sesame seeds until combined.

3. On a parchment-lined baking sheet, arrange the eggplant slices in a single layer.

4. Brush the eggplant slices with the miso glaze.

5. Drizzle the vegetable oil over the eggplant slices.

6. Bake for 25-30 minutes, or until the eggplant is tender and golden brown.

7. Serve warm.

Nutritional Value (Per Serving)

Calories: 140

Carbohydrates: 11g

Fat: 6g

Protein: 3g

Sodium: 500mg

Fiber: 4g

Steamed Bok Choy

Prep time: 5 minutes

Cook time: 5 minutes

Total time: 10 minutes

Ingredients

- 1 head of bok choy, washed and trimmed

- 1 tablespoon of olive oil

- 1 teaspoon of garlic, minced

- Salt and pepper to taste

Instructions

1. Fill a large pot with 1 inch of water and place a steamer basket inside.

2. Bring the water to a boil, then reduce the heat to medium-low.

3. Place the bok choy in the steamer basket and cover with a lid.

4. Steam for 5 minutes, or until the bok choy is tender.

5. Remove the bok choy from the steamer basket and transfer to a plate.

6. Drizzle with olive oil, garlic, salt, and pepper.

7. Serve and enjoy!

Nutritional Value (per serving)

Calories: 70

Fat: 4 g

Carbohydrates: 6 g

Protein: 3 g

Fiber: 2 g

Sugar: 2 g

Sodium: 120 mg

Grilled Tofu and Vegetables

Ingredients

- 1 package of extra firm tofu

- 1 red bell pepper, sliced

- 1 zucchini, sliced

- 1 yellow squash, sliced

- 2 tablespoons of olive oil

- Salt and pepper to taste

Instructions

1. Preheat a grill over medium-high heat.

2. Cut the tofu into 1-inch cubes and place in a large bowl.

3. Add the sliced vegetables along with the olive oil, salt, and pepper to the bowl and mix until the vegetables are evenly coated.

4. Place the vegetables and tofu on the grill and cook for 10 minutes, flipping once halfway through.

5. Serve the grilled tofu and vegetables with your favorite side dish.

Nutritional Value

Calories: 210

Carbohydrates: 8g

Protein: 13g

Fat: 12g

Sodium: 222mg

Asian-Style Asparagus and Mushrooms

Time Required: 10 minutes

Ingredients

-1 lb. fresh asparagus, trimmed and cut into 1-inch pieces

-2 cups sliced mushrooms

-1 tablespoon olive oil

-1 tablespoon low-sodium soy sauce

-2 cloves garlic, minced

-1 teaspoon fresh grated ginger

-1 tablespoon sesame oil

-1 tablespoon toasted sesame seeds

Instructions

1. Heat olive oil in a large pot over medium-high heat.

2. Add asparagus and mushrooms and cook for 5 minutes, stirring occasionally.

3. Add soy sauce, garlic, ginger, and sesame oil and cook for an additional 2 minutes.

4. Remove from heat and stir in toasted sesame seeds.

5. Serve hot.

Nutritional Value (per serving)

Calories: 85 kcal

Protein: 3 g

Carbohydrates: 5 g

Fat: 6 g

Fiber: 2 g

Sugar: 2 g

Sesame-Ginger Broccoli

Prep Time: 10 minutes

Cook Time: 10 minutes

Total Time: 20 minutes

Ingredients

- 2 heads of broccoli, cut into florets

- 2 tablespoons of sesame oil

- 2 tablespoons of grated ginger

- 1 tablespoon of minced garlic

- 2 tablespoons of soy sauce

- 2 tablespoons of sesame seeds

- Salt and pepper to taste

Instructions

1. Preheat oven to 375°F.

2. Grease a baking sheet with sesame oil.

3. Place broccoli florets on baking sheet and season with salt and pepper.

4. Roast broccoli in preheated oven for 8 to 10 minutes, or until tender.

5. In a separate bowl, mix together sesame oil, ginger, garlic, soy sauce, and sesame seeds.

6. Remove broccoli from oven and coat with sesame oil mixture.

7. Return broccoli to oven and bake for an additional 2 minutes.

8. Serve hot.

Nutritional Value

Calories: 158

Fat: 10.2g

Carbohydrates: 12.4g

Protein: 6.2g

Fiber: 3.5g

Asian-Style Green Bean Salad

Servings: 2

Total Time: 20 minutes

Nutritional Values

Calories: 134

Carbohydrates: 25 g

Protein: 4 g

Fat: 6 g

Ingredients

- 1 tablespoon sesame oil
- 1 teaspoon minced garlic
- 1 tablespoon rice vinegar
- 1 teaspoon honey
- 1 teaspoon low-sodium soy sauce
- 1/2 teaspoon ground ginger
- 1/4 teaspoon red pepper flakes
- 1/4 teaspoon salt

- 1/4 teaspoon black pepper
- 2 cups fresh green beans, trimmed and halved
- 2 teaspoons sesame seeds

Instructions

1. Heat sesame oil in a large pot over medium-high heat. Add garlic and cook for 30 seconds, stirring constantly.

2. In a small bowl, whisk together the rice vinegar, honey, soy sauce, ginger, red pepper flakes, salt, and pepper.

3. Add green beans to the skillet and toss to coat. Cook for 5 minutes, stirring occasionally.

4. Pour the vinegar mixture over the green beans and toss to coat. Cook for another 5 minutes, stirring occasionally.

5. Sprinkle with sesame seeds and serve.

Stir-Fried Spinach with Garlic

Time Required: 10 minutes

Servings: 2

Ingredients

- 2 tablespoons olive oil

- 2 cloves garlic, minced

- 2 bunches fresh spinach, washed and chopped

- Salt and pepper to taste

Instructions

1. Heat the olive oil in a large skillet over medium-high heat.

2. Add the garlic and sauté for 1 minute.

3. Add the spinach and cook, stirring frequently, for 5 minutes or until the spinach is wilted.

4. Season with salt and pepper to taste.

5. Serve hot. Enjoy!

Nutrition (per serving)

Calories: 125

Carbohydrates: 8 g

Protein: 5 g

Fat: 9 g

Asian-Style Cucumber Salad

Servings: 4

Total Time: 15 minutes

Ingredients

- 2 cucumbers, peeled and sliced
- 2 tablespoons rice vinegar
- 1 teaspoon grated ginger
- 1 teaspoon sesame oil
- 1 tablespoon low-sodium soy sauce
- 2 tablespoons chopped scallions
- 2 tablespoons sesame seeds
- 1 teaspoon honey
- Salt and pepper, to taste

Instructions

1. In a large bowl, combine the cucumbers, rice vinegar, ginger, sesame oil, soy sauce, scallions, sesame seeds, honey, salt, and pepper.

2. Toss to combine.

3. Serve immediately.

Nutritional Value (per serving)

Calories: 60

Fat: 3g;

Cholesterol: 0mg

Sodium: 200mg

Carbohydrates: 7g

Fiber: 2g;

Protein: 2g

Sugar: 4g

Tofu and Vegetable Lettuce Wraps

Prep Time: 10 minutes

Cook Time: 15 minutes

Total Time: 25 minutes

Servings: 4

Ingredients

- 1 block of extra firm tofu, drained and diced

- 2 tablespoons of olive oil

- 2 cloves of garlic, minced

- 2 bell peppers, diced

- 2 cups of mushrooms, diced

- ½ cup of diced onion

- 1 teaspoon of ground ginger

- 1 teaspoon of ground cumin

- 1 teaspoon of chili powder

- Salt and pepper, to taste

- 4 large lettuce leaves

- 2 tablespoons of sesame seeds

- 4 tablespoons of soy sauce

Instructions

1. Heat a large skillet over medium heat and add the olive oil.

2. Add in the garlic, bell peppers, mushrooms and onion and cook for 3-4 minutes until the vegetables are softened.

3. Add in the diced tofu and season with the ginger, cumin, chili powder, salt and pepper. Cook for an additional 5 minutes, stirring occasionally.

4. Divide the tofu and vegetable mixture among the lettuce leaves and top with the sesame seeds and soy sauce.

5. Serve warm and enjoy!

Nutrition per Serving

Calories: 152

Fat: 8g

Carbohydrates: 9g

Protein: 11g

Sweet Potato Fries with the Asian-Style Dipping Sauce

prep time: 10 mins

cook time: 30 mins

servings: 4

Ingredients

- 2 large sweet potatoes, cut into 1/4-inch thick slices

- 2 tablespoons olive oil

- 1/2 teaspoon garlic powder

- 1/4 teaspoon paprika

- Salt and pepper, to taste

- For the Asian-Style Dipping Sauce:

- 1/4 cup soy sauce

- 2 tablespoons rice vinegar

- 2 tablespoons honey

- 1 teaspoon sesame oil

- 1/2 teaspoon freshly grated ginger

Instructions

1. Preheat oven to 425 degrees F.

2. Line a baking sheet with parchment paper.

3. In a large bowl, combine the sweet potatoes, olive oil, garlic powder, paprika, salt and pepper. Toss to combine.

4. Spread the sweet potatoes out on the prepared baking sheet in a single layer.

5. Bake in preheated oven for 25-30 minutes, flipping once halfway through cooking, until golden brown and crispy.

6. Meanwhile, make the Asian-style dipping sauce. In a medium bowl, whisk together the soy sauce, rice vinegar, honey, sesame oil, and ginger.

7. Serve the sweet potato fries with the Asian-style dipping sauce. Enjoy!

Nutritional Value per Serving

Calories: 267

Fat: 10 g

Carbohydrates: 40 g

Fiber: 4 g

Protein: 4 g

Sodium: 514 mg

Sugar: 5 g

Grilled Eggplant with Miso Sauce

Servings: 4

Prep Time: 10 minutes

Cook Time: 20 minutes

Ingredients

- 2 large eggplants, sliced into 1/4-inch thick rounds

- 2 tablespoons olive oil

- 2 tablespoons white miso paste

- 1 tablespoon rice vinegar

- 1 teaspoon sesame oil

- 1 teaspoon honey

- 2 cloves garlic, minced

- 2 tablespoons sesame seeds

Instructions

1. Preheat your grill to medium-high heat.

2. Brush the eggplant slices with the olive oil and season with salt and pepper.

3. Grill the eggplant slices for about 10 minutes, flipping once, until they are tender and lightly charred.

4. In a small bowl, whisk together the miso paste, rice vinegar, sesame oil, honey, garlic, and sesame seeds.

5. Brush the grilled eggplant slices with the miso sauce and cook for an additional 5 minutes, until the sauce is lightly charred.

6. Serve the eggplant slices warm with additional miso sauce, if desired.

Nutritional Value

Calories: 121

Fat: 7.2g

Carbohydrates: 12.2g

Protein: 2.3g

Fiber: 4.3g

Grilled Asian-Style Squash

Prep Time: 10 minutes

Cook Time: 8 minutes

Total Time: 18 minutes

Ingredients

- 1 large squash, sliced into 1/2-inch thick slices

- 2 tablespoons sesame oil

- 2 tablespoons low-sodium soy sauce

- 2 teaspoons freshly grated ginger

- 2 cloves garlic, minced

- 1 teaspoon chili flakes

- 2 tablespoons freshly chopped cilantro

- Salt and pepper to taste

Instructions

1. Preheat your grill over medium-high heat.

2. Place the squash slices in a large bowl and season with salt and pepper.

3. In a small bowl, combine the sesame oil, soy sauce, ginger, garlic, chili flakes, and cilantro. Mix until combined.

4. Pour the mixture over the squash and toss until the squash is evenly coated.

5. Place the squash slices on the preheated grill and cook for about 4 minutes per side, or until the squash is tender and lightly charred.

6. Serve warm with your favorite side dish!

Nutritional Value (per serving)

Calories: 98

Fat: 5.7 g

Carbohydrates: 9.4 g

Protein: 2.2 g

Fiber: 2.2 g

Sugar: 4.2 g

Asian-Style Marinated Tofu

Prep Time: 15 minutes

Cook Time: 15 minutes

Total Time: 30 minutes

Ingredients

- 1 block extra-firm tofu, drained and cubed
- 2 tablespoons low-sodium soy sauce
- 2 tablespoons honey
- 1 tablespoon rice vinegar
- 1 tablespoon sesame oil
- 1 teaspoon grated fresh ginger
- 1 teaspoon garlic powder
- 1 teaspoon ground black pepper

Instructions

1. Preheat your oven to 375 degrees Fahrenheit.

2. In a medium bowl, whisk together soy sauce, honey, rice vinegar, sesame oil, ginger, garlic powder, and black pepper until well combined.

3. Add cubed tofu to the mixture and stir until the tofu is evenly coated.

4. Place the tofu on a parchment-lined baking sheet and bake for 15 minutes, flipping once halfway through.

5. Serve over brown rice or quinoa and enjoy!

Nutritional Value

Calories: 191

Fat: 11g

Carbohydrates: 14g

Protein: 9g

Fiber: 1g

Sugar: 10g

Stir-Fried Chinese Broccoli

Time Required: 15 minutes

Ingredients

- 2 tablespoons low-sodium soy sauce

- 2 teaspoons honey

- 2 teaspoons grated fresh ginger

- 2 cloves garlic, minced

- 1 teaspoon sesame oil

- 1 head Chinese broccoli, trimmed and cut into 1-inch pieces

- 2 tablespoons vegetable oil

Instructions

1. In a small bowl, whisk together the soy sauce, honey, ginger, garlic, and sesame oil.

2. Heat the vegetable oil in a large pot over medium-high heat. Add the Chinese broccoli and stir-fry for 2-3 minutes until tender.

3. Add the soy sauce mixture and stir-fry for an additional 2 minutes.

4. Serve hot. Enjoy!

Nutritional Value

Calories: 97

Carbs: 7.1 g

Fat: 5.3 g

Protein: 5.3 g

Grilled Tofu and Peppers

Servings: 4

Prep Time: 10 minutes

Cook Time: 20 minutes

Total Time: 30 minutes

Ingredients

- 1 block extra-firm tofu, drained and cut into 8 equal slices
- 2 bell peppers, sliced into thin strips
- 2 tablespoons olive oil
- 1 teaspoon garlic powder
- 1 teaspoon Italian seasoning
- Salt and pepper to taste

Instructions

1. Preheat grill to medium-high heat.

2. Place the tofu slices in a shallow dish and drizzle with olive oil. Sprinkle with garlic powder, Italian seasoning, salt, and pepper. Mix together and let sit for 10 minutes.

3. Place the peppers on a large sheet of aluminum foil. Drizzle with remaining olive oil, salt, and pepper.

4. Place the tofu slices and peppers on the preheated grill. Grill for 10 minutes, flipping once halfway through.

5. Remove from grill and serve immediately.

Nutritional Value

Calories: 154

Protein: 11g

Carbohydrates: 5g

Fat: 11g

Fiber: 2g

Sugar: 2g

Asian-Style Quinoa Salad

Servings: 4

Total Time: 45 minutes

Ingredients

-1 cup uncooked quinoa

-2 cups vegetable broth

-2 tablespoons sesame oil

-1/2 cup diced red bell pepper

-1/2 cup diced carrots

-1/4 cup diced green onions

-1 tablespoon fresh ginger, grated

-1/4 cup soy sauce

-2 tablespoons rice vinegar

-1/2 teaspoon garlic powder

-2 tablespoons sesame seeds

Instructions

1. In a saucepan, bring the vegetable broth to a boil.

2. Add the quinoa and reduce heat to low. Cover and simmer for 15 minutes, or until the quinoa is cooked.

3. In a large bowl, combine the cooked quinoa, sesame oil, red bell pepper, carrots, green onions, ginger, soy sauce, rice vinegar, and garlic powder.

4. Gently mix together and sprinkle with sesame seeds.

5. Serve warm or chilled.

Nutritional Value (per serving)

Calories: 230

Fat: 8g

Carbohydrates: 29g

Protein: 7g

Fiber: 4g

Asian-Style Tomato and Cucumber Salad

Time Required: 15 minutes

Servings: 4

Ingredients

- 2 tomatoes, diced
- 1 cucumber, diced
- 2 tablespoons rice vinegar
- 2 teaspoons soy sauce

- 1 teaspoon sesame oil
- 1 teaspoon honey
- 1 teaspoon freshly grated ginger
- 2 tablespoons fresh cilantro, chopped
- 1 garlic clove, minced

Instructions

1. In a medium bowl, combine the diced tomatoes and cucumber.

2. In a small bowl, whisk together the rice vinegar, soy sauce, sesame oil, honey, ginger, cilantro, and garlic.

3. Pour the dressing over the tomatoes and cucumbers and mix until evenly coated.

4. Serve immediately or refrigerate until ready to serve. Enjoy!

Asian-Style Egg Drop Soup

Time Required: 20 minutes

Ingredients

- 2 cups low-sodium chicken broth
- 1 tablespoon reduced-sodium soy sauce

- 2 teaspoons freshly grated ginger

- 1 teaspoon sesame oil

- 1/2 cup thinly sliced mushrooms

- 1/4 cup sliced green onions

- 1/4 cup frozen corn

- 2 large egg whites, lightly beaten

- 1 tablespoon chopped fresh cilantro

Instructions

1. In a large saucepan, bring chicken broth, soy sauce, ginger, and sesame oil to a boil over medium-high heat.

2. Add mushrooms, green onions, and corn. Reduce heat to medium-low and simmer for 8-10 minutes, stirring occasionally.

3. Slowly pour the egg whites into the soup while stirring. Cook for 1-2 minutes, until the eggs are cooked.

4. Remove from heat and stir in cilantro. Serve warm. Enjoy!

Nutritional Value (per serving)

Calories: 105 kcal

Carbohydrates: 10.3 g

Protein: 7.2 g

Fat: 3.3 g

Asian-Style Cabbage and Potato Soup

Prep Time: 10 minutes

Cook Time: 25 minutes

Total Time: 35 minutes

Servings: 6

Ingredients

- 2 tablespoons sesame oil
- 1 cup diced onion
- 2 cloves garlic, minced
- 4 cups low-sodium vegetable broth
- 2 cups diced potatoes
- 2 cups shredded cabbage
- 1 teaspoon ground ginger
- 2 tablespoons low-sodium soy sauce
- 1 teaspoon rice vinegar

- 2 tablespoons chopped fresh cilantro

Instructions

1. Heat the sesame oil in a large pot over medium-high heat.

2. Add the onion and garlic and cook, stirring occasionally, until the onion is translucent, about 5 minutes.

3. Add the vegetable broth, potatoes, cabbage, ginger, soy sauce and rice vinegar. Boil the mixture, then reduce the heat to low. Simmer, stirring occasionally, until the potatoes are tender, about 20 minutes.

4. Remove the soup from the heat and stir in the cilantro. Serve warm.

Nutritional Value (per serving)

Calories: 86

Protein: 2g

Total Fat: 5g

Saturated Fat: 1g

Carbohydrates: 8g

Fiber: 2g

Sugar: 2g

Cholesterol: 0mg

Sodium: 437mg

Asian-Style Noodle Soup

Prep time: 10 minutes

Cook time: 20 minutes

Total time: 30 minutes

Servings: 4

Nutritional Value

Calories: 414

Carbohydrates: 64 g

Fat: 11 g

Protein: 13 g

Ingredients

- 2 tablespoons peanut oil

- 1 onion, diced

- 2 garlic cloves, minced

- 2 tablespoons grated ginger

- 6 cups low-sodium vegetable broth

- 2 tablespoons reduced-sodium soy sauce

- 2 tablespoons rice vinegar

- 2 tablespoons sesame oil

- 2 carrots, peeled and julienned

- 2 celery stalks, julienned

- 2 cups bean sprouts

- 4 ounces rice noodles

- 2 green onions, thinly sliced

Instructions

1. Heat the peanut oil in a large pot over medium heat.

2. Add the onion and garlic and cook until softened, about 5 minutes.

3. Add the ginger, broth, soy sauce, rice vinegar, and sesame oil and bring to a boil.

4. Reduce the heat and simmer for 10 minutes.

5. Add the carrots, celery, and bean sprouts and simmer for an additional 5 minutes.

6. Add the rice noodles and cook until just tender, about 2 minutes.

7. Add the green onions, salt, and pepper.

8. Serve the soup hot. Enjoy!

Main Dishes

Diabetes is a serious medical condition that affects millions of people around the world, and the challenge of managing it can be especially difficult for those who enjoy delicious Asian cuisine. Fortunately, with some careful planning and creativity, it is possible to enjoy delicious, diabetes-friendly Asian main dishes that have all the flavor, texture, and variety of traditional recipes. One of the most important steps in preparing diabetes-friendly Asian main dishes is to choose ingredients wisely. Many traditional Asian dishes rely heavily on sodium-rich sauces and seasonings, as well as a large amount of added sugar. While these ingredients can add flavor and texture to a dish, they can also significantly increase the risk of diabetes when eaten in large amounts.

Instead, opt for natural, low-sodium ingredients like fresh vegetables, lean proteins, and healthy fats to ensure that your dish is diabetes-friendly without sacrificing flavor. When it comes to cooking, there are several ways to create delicious diabetes-friendly Asian main dishes. Consider stir-frying, steaming, and roasting as healthy cooking methods that require little to no added fat or sugar. Start by prepping your ingredients, such as dicing vegetables, slicing proteins, and pre-cooking starches like rice. Then, heat a wok or large skillet over medium-high heat and add a small amount of oil. Add vegetables, proteins, and seasonings and cook for several minutes until vegetables are tender and proteins are cooked through. Serve over cooked rice or noodles. For those looking for a flavorful but diabetes-friendly Asian main dish, consider making a vegetable-based stir-fry. Start by prepping a variety of vegetables such as bell peppers, carrots, mushrooms, and snow peas. Then, heat a wok or large skillet over medium-high heat and add a small amount of oil. Add the vegetables and seasonings such as garlic, ginger, and soy sauce and cook for several minutes until vegetables are tender. Serve over cooked rice or noodles. For a protein-packed main dish, try a chicken and vegetable stir-fry. Start by prepping a variety of vegetables such as bell peppers, carrots, mushrooms, and snow peas. Then, heat a wok or large skillet over medium-high heat and add a small amount of oil.

Add the chicken and seasonings such as garlic, ginger, and soy sauce and cook for several minutes until chicken is cooked through. Add the vegetables and cook for a few more minutes until vegetables are tender. Serve over cooked rice or noodles. Finally, for a lighter option, consider a vegetable-based soup. Start by prepping a variety of vegetables such as carrots, mushrooms, and snow peas. Then, heat a large pot over medium-high heat and add a small amount of oil. Add the vegetables and seasonings such as garlic, ginger, and soy sauce and cook for several minutes until vegetables are tender. Add broth or water and bring to a boil. Simmer for several minutes, then add cooked noodles and cook until noodles are tender.

Serve hot. With some careful planning and creativity, it is possible to enjoy delicious, diabetes-friendly Asian main dishes that have all the flavor and texture of traditional recipes.

By choosing low-sodium ingredients and healthy cooking methods, you can create delicious, diabetes-friendly dishes that are sure to please.

Vegetable Stir-Fry

Time Required: 20 minutes

Ingredients

-1 tablespoon olive oil

-1 onion, diced

-1 bell pepper, diced

-1 cup broccoli florets

-1 cup sliced mushrooms

-1 cup diced carrots

-1 cup diced celery

-2 cloves garlic, minced

-2 tablespoons reduced-sodium soy sauce

Instructions

1. Heat oil in a large pot over medium heat.

2. Add the onion, bell pepper, broccoli, mushrooms, carrots, celery, and garlic. Cook until the vegetables are tender, about 10 minutes.

3. Add the soy sauce and stir to combine. Cook for another 2-3 minutes, until the vegetables are cooked through.

4. Serve the stir-fry warm.

Nutritional Value

Calories: 115

Fat: 5 g

Carbohydrates: 15 g

Fiber: 5 g

Protein: 4 g

Sodium: 394 mg

Brown Rice Bowl with Vegetables

Prep Time: 10 minutes

Cook Time: 25 minutes

Total Time: 35 minutes

Servings: 4

Nutritional Value

Calories: 320

Carbohydrates: 46 g

Fiber: 7 g

Protein: 8 g

Fat: 6 g

Ingredients

2 cups brown rice

1 cup diced carrots

1 cup diced bell peppers

1 cup diced mushrooms

1/2 cup diced red onion

1 teaspoon olive oil

1/2 teaspoon garlic powder

1/2 teaspoon onion powder

1/2 teaspoon salt

1/4 teaspoon black pepper

Instructions

1. In a medium saucepan, bring 2 cups of water to a boil.

2. Add the brown rice and reduce the heat to low. Simmer for 25 minutes or until the rice is cooked through.

3. Meanwhile, in a separate pan, heat the olive oil over medium heat.

4. Add the carrots, bell peppers, mushrooms, and red onion.

5. Cook for about 10 minutes, stirring occasionally, until the vegetables are crisp-tender.

6. Add the garlic powder, onion powder, salt, and black pepper and stir to combine.

7. When the rice is cooked, divide it into four servings and top each with the sautéed vegetables.

Tofu and Veggie Pad Thai

Time Required: 30 minutes

Servings: 4

Nutritional Value (Per Serving)

Calories: 350

Protein: 17 g

Total Fat: 9 g

Carbohydrates: 46 g

Fiber: 6 g

Sugar: 7 g

Ingredients

- 1 package firm tofu, pressed and cubed
- 2 tablespoons olive oil
- 4 cloves garlic, minced
- 2 cups broccoli florets
- 1 red bell pepper, diced
- 1 cup snow peas
- 2 tablespoons low-sodium soy sauce
- 2 tablespoons lime juice
- 2 tablespoons peanut butter
- 1 tablespoon honey

- 1 teaspoon chili paste

- 2 tablespoons chopped peanuts

- 4 ounces rice noodles

Instructions

1. Heat the olive oil in a large skillet over medium heat. Add the garlic and cook for 1 minute.

2. Add the tofu cubes, broccoli, bell pepper, and snow peas and cook for 5 minutes.

3. Meanwhile, in a small bowl, whisk together the soy sauce, lime juice, peanut butter, honey, and chili paste.

4. Pour the sauce into the skillet and cook for an additional 5 minutes.

5. Add the peanuts and cook for 1 minute.

6. Meanwhile, cook the rice noodles according to package instructions.

7. Once the noodles are cooked, add them to the skillet and toss to combine.

8. Serve the pad thai warm with additional chopped peanuts, if desired. Enjoy!

Egg Drop Soup

Time Required: 10 minutes

Servings: 4

Ingredients

- 4 cups of low-sodium vegetable broth

- 1 teaspoon of minced garlic

- 1 tablespoon of freshly grated ginger

- 2 tablespoons of low-sodium soy sauce

- 1 teaspoon of sesame oil

- 2 teaspoons of cornstarch

- 2 eggs, lightly beaten

- 2 green onions, thinly sliced

Instructions

1. In a large pot, add the vegetable broth, garlic, ginger, soy sauce, and sesame oil. Bring to a boil over medium-high heat.

2. Once boiling, reduce the heat to medium-low and simmer for 5 minutes.

3. In a small bowl, mix together the cornstarch and 2 tablespoons of water until it forms a paste.

4. Slowly pour the cornstarch mixture into the soup, stirring constantly. Simmer for 1 minute.

5. Slowly pour in the beaten eggs, stirring in a figure-eight motion. Cook for 1 minute.

6. Turn off the heat and stir in the green onions.

7. Serve hot.

Nutritional Value

Calories: 59 kcal

Protein: 4g

Carbohydrates: 4g

Fat: 2g

Saturated Fat: 0.5g

Cholesterol: 64mg

Sodium: 590mg

Fiber: 0.5g

Sugar: 1g

Sushi rolls with cucumber, avocado and pickled ginger

Time Required: 25 minutes

Ingredients

- 3 tablespoons sushi rice

- 1/2 cucumber, thinly sliced

- 1/2 avocado, thinly sliced

- 2 tablespoons pickled ginger

- 2 sheets nori seaweed

- Rice vinegar

Instructions

1. Cook the sushi rice according to package instructions. Once cooked, spread the rice over a large plate and sprinkle with a few drops of rice vinegar.

2. Take a sheet of nori seaweed and lay it on a bamboo rolling mat. Spread a layer of sushi rice over the nori seaweed, leaving a 1/2 inch margin of nori uncovered at the top.

3. Arrange the cucumber slices and avocado slices over the sushi rice in a single layer.

4. Sprinkle the pickled ginger over the cucumber and avocado.

5. Carefully roll the sushi from the bottom up with the bamboo rolling mat, pressing firmly to ensure the roll is tight.

6. Cut the roll into 8 pieces using a sharp knife.

7. Serve and enjoy!

Nutritional Value

Calories: 100

Fat: 4g

Carbohydrates: 15g

Protein: 2g

Fiber: 4g

Grilled Fish with Steamed Vegetables

Prep Time: 20 minutes

Cook Time: 10 minutes

Total Time: 30 minutes

Servings: 4

Ingredients

- 4 (4-ounce) fish fillets

- 2 tablespoons olive oil

- 2 tablespoons fresh lemon juice

- 2 teaspoons minced garlic

- 2 teaspoons dried oregano

- Salt and pepper, to taste

- 2 cups assorted vegetables (such as broccoli, carrots, and red peppers), chopped

- 2 tablespoons chopped fresh parsley

Instructions

1. Preheat grill to medium-high heat.

2. In a medium bowl, combine olive oil, lemon juice, garlic, oregano, salt and pepper.

3. Place fish in the marinade and let sit for 10 minutes.

4. Place vegetables in a steamer over boiling water and steam for 5 minutes.

5. Grill fish for 4-5 minutes per side, or until cooked through.

6. Serve grilled fish with steamed vegetables and garnish with parsley. Enjoy!

Nutritional Value Per Serving

Calories: 165

Protein: 23g

Fat: 7g

Carbohydrates: 9g

Vegetable Fried Rice

Time Required: 15 minutes

Nutritional Value

Calories: 219 kcal

Fat: 10 g

Carbohydrates: 27 g

Protein: 5 g

Sodium: 522 mg

Fiber: 5 g

Ingredients

1/4 cup cooked brown rice

2 tablespoons olive oil

1/2 cup diced onion

1/2 cup diced carrots

1/2 cup diced bell peppers

1/2 cup diced mushrooms

1/2 cup diced celery

1 cup diced green beans

2 cloves of garlic, minced

2 tablespoons reduced sodium soy sauce

1 teaspoon sesame oil

Instructions

1. Heat the olive oil in a large pot over medium-high heat.

2. Add the onions, carrots, bell peppers, mushrooms, celery, and green beans. Cook, stirring occasionally, until the vegetables are softened, about 5 minutes.

3. Add the garlic and cooked brown rice. Cook, stirring occasionally, for 2 minutes.

4. Put the soy sauce and sesame oil. Cook, stirring occasionally, for 2 minutes, or until the vegetables are cooked through.

5. Serve Hot.

Chicken Teriyaki with Steamed Vegetables

Ingredients

- 2 chicken breasts

- 2 tablespoons soy sauce

- 2 tablespoons of honey

- 2 cloves of garlic, minced

- 1 teaspoon of fresh ginger, minced

- 1 teaspoon of sesame oil

- 1 head of broccoli

- 1 red pepper

- 1 carrot

- 2 cups of brown rice

Instructions

1. In a medium bowl, combine the soy sauce, honey, garlic, ginger, and sesame oil. Mix until blended.

2. Place chicken breasts in the marinade and let sit for 15-20 minutes.

3. While the chicken is marinating, prepare the vegetables. Chop the broccoli, red pepper, and carrot into bite-size pieces.

4. Heat a large pot over medium-high heat. Add the vegetables to the skillet and cook for 8-10 minutes, stirring occasionally.

5. Add the chicken and marinade to the skillet and cook for an additional 8-10 minutes, stirring occasionally.

6. While the chicken is cooking, prepare the brown rice according to the package instructions.

7. Serve the chicken and vegetables over the brown rice. Enjoy!

Nutritional Value

Servings: 4

Calories: 439

Fat: 11g

Carbohydrates: 54g

Protein: 31g

Fiber: 5g

Miso Soup with Tofu, Seaweed, and Mushrooms

Ingredients

- 2 tablespoons of miso paste

- 1 teaspoon of sesame oil

- 2 cups of vegetable broth

- 2 cups of diced tofu

- 1 cup of chopped seaweed

- 1 cup of sliced mushrooms

- 2 tablespoons of soy sauce

Instructions

1. Heat the sesame oil in a large pot over medium heat.

2. Add the tofu and cook until lightly browned and crispy, about 5 minutes.

3. Add the seaweed, mushrooms, and vegetable broth and bring to a boil.

4. Reduce heat to low and simmer for 10 minutes.

5. Stir in the miso paste and soy sauce and simmer for an additional 5 minutes.

6. Serve hot.

Nutritional Value

Calories: 150

Protein: 10g

Fat: 8g

Carbohydrates: 10g

Sodium: 650mg

Fiber: 2g

Sugars: 2g

Vegetable Lo Mein

Prep time: 10 minutes

Cook time: 10 minutes

Total time: 20 minutes

Ingredients

- 8 ounces whole wheat spaghetti

- 2 tablespoons sesame oil

- 2 cloves garlic, minced

- 2 carrots, thinly sliced

- 1 red bell pepper, julienned

- 2 stalks celery, thinly sliced

- 1/2 cup broccoli florets

- 2 tablespoons low sodium soy sauce

- 1 tablespoon honey

- 1 teaspoon freshly grated ginger

- 1/4 teaspoon red pepper flakes

Instructions

1. Cook the spaghetti according to package instructions.

2. Heat the sesame oil in a large skillet over medium-high heat. Add the garlic and cook until fragrant, about 1-2 minutes.

3. Add the carrots, bell pepper, celery, and broccoli to the skillet and cook until crisp-tender, about 5 minutes.

4. In a small bowl, whisk together the soy sauce, honey, ginger, and red pepper flakes.

5. Add the cooked spaghetti to the skillet and pour the sauce over the top. Cook until the sauce is heated through and the vegetables are fully cooked, about 2-3 minutes.

6. Serve immediately.

Nutritional Value

Calories: 300

Protein: 8 grams

Carbohydrates: 54 grams

Fat: 6 grams

Fiber: 8 grams

Grilled Chicken and Vegetable Skewers

Time Required: 30 minutes

Nutritional Value

Calories: 315 kcal

Carbohydrates: 6.4 g

Protein: 28.4 g

Fat: 15.6 g

Ingredients

- 1 lb. boneless, skinless, chicken breasts, cut into 1 inch cubes
- 1 cup bell peppers, cut into 1 inch pieces

- 1 cup zucchini, cut into 1 inch pieces

- 1 cup red onions, cut into 1 inch pieces

- 2 tablespoons olive oil

- 1 teaspoon garlic powder

- 1 teaspoon dried oregano

- 1 teaspoon dried basil

- Salt and pepper to taste

Instructions

1. Preheat your grill to medium-high heat.

2. In a large bowl, combine the chicken, bell peppers, zucchini and red onions.

3. Drizzle the vegetables and chicken with the olive oil and season with the garlic powder, oregano, basil, salt and pepper.

4. Toss everything together until the vegetables and chicken are evenly coated.

5. Place the vegetables and chicken onto 8-10 skewers and place on the preheated grill.

6. Grill for 8-10 minutes, flipping the skewers halfway through, until the chicken is cooked through and the vegetables are tender.

7. Serve the skewers with your favorite side dish. Enjoy!

Thai Yellow Curry with Vegetables

Servings: 4

Prep Time: 10 minutes

Cook Time: 20 minutes

Ingredients

- 2 tablespoons coconut oil

- 1 teaspoon garlic, minced

- 1 teaspoon ginger, minced

- 1/2 teaspoon chili paste

- 2 tablespoons yellow curry powder

- 2 tablespoons fish sauce

- 1/2 teaspoon brown sugar

- 2 cups vegetable broth

- 1/2 cup light coconut milk

- 2 cups mixed vegetables, such as bell peppers, carrots, zucchini, mushrooms

- 2 tablespoons fresh basil, chopped

- 2 tablespoons fresh cilantro, chopped

- Salt and pepper, to taste

Directions

1. Heat coconut oil in a large pan at medium heat. Add garlic and ginger and sauté for 2 minutes.

2. Add chili paste, curry powder, fish sauce, and brown sugar and cook for 1 minute.

3. Add vegetable broth, light coconut milk, and mixed vegetables and bring to a boil. Reduce heat to low and simmer for 10 minutes.

4. Add basil and cilantro and season with salt and pepper to taste. Simmer for an additional 5 minutes.

Nutritional Value (per serving)

Calories: 197

Fat: 11.9 g

Carbohydrates: 16.6 g

Protein: 4.8 g

Fiber: 3.2 g

Sugar: 5.2 g

Chicken and Vegetable Tempura

Servings: 4

Time Required: 45 minutes

Ingredients

- 1 lb. boneless skinless chicken breasts, cut into 1-inch cubes
- 2 cups assorted vegetables, such as zucchini, bell peppers, and mushrooms, cut into 1-inch cubes
- 2 cups whole wheat flour
- 2 eggs
- 2 cups cold sparkling water
- 1 teaspoon garlic powder
- 1 teaspoon onion powder
- 1 teaspoon smoked paprika
- 1 teaspoon sea salt
- Vegetable oil, for frying

Instructions

1. Heat the oil in a heavy-bottomed pot to 350°F.

2. In a large bowl, combine the flour, eggs, sparkling water, garlic powder, onion powder, smoked paprika, and sea salt. Whisk until the batter is smooth.

3. Dip the chicken and vegetables into the batter to coat.

4. Carefully drop the battered chicken and vegetables into the preheated oil. Fry for 4-5 minutes, until golden brown and crispy.

5. Remove the tempura from the oil and drain on a paper towel-lined plate.

6. Serve with your most preferred dipping sauce and enjoy!

Nutritional Value

Calories: 246

Fat: 11g

Carbohydrates: 20g

Protein: 17g

Vegetable-Filled Egg Rolls

Servings: 12

Prep Time: 20 minutes

Cook Time: 15 minutes

Total Time: 35 minutes

Ingredients

- 3 tablespoons of vegetable oil

- 4 cloves of garlic, minced

- 2 cups of shredded cabbage

- 2 cups of shredded carrots

- 2 cups of mushrooms, diced

- 1 teaspoon of freshly grated ginger

- 1 teaspoon of toasted sesame oil

- 4 tablespoons of low-sodium soy sauce

- 1 teaspoon of sugar

- 12 egg roll wrappers

Instructions

1. Heat the vegetable oil in a large skillet over medium heat.

2. Add the garlic and cook for 1 minute.

3. Add the cabbage, carrots, mushrooms, ginger, and sesame oil and cook for 5 minutes, stirring occasionally.

4. Add the soy sauce and sugar and cook for another 3 minutes.

5. Remove the skillet from the heat and let the mixture cool.

6. Place one egg roll wrapper on a clean plane. Place 2 tablespoons of the vegetable mixture in the center of the wrapper.

7. Fold the bottom corner of the wrapper over the filling, then fold in the sides.

8. Moisten the top corner of the wrapper with water and roll it over the filling.

9. Repeat with the remaining wrappers and filling.

10. Heat enough oil in a large skillet over medium-high heat to cover the bottom of the pan.

11. Carefully add the egg rolls to the pan and cook for 3-4 minutes per side, or until golden brown.

12. Remove the egg rolls from the pan and let them cool for a few minutes before serving.

Nutritional Value

Calories: 90

Fat: 4g

Carbohydrates: 11g

Protein: 2g

Fiber: 2g

Vegetable Ramen

Prep time: 15 minutes

Cook time: 10 minutes

Total time: 25 minutes

Ingredients

-1 tablespoon sesame oil

-1 tablespoon grated ginger

-2 cloves garlic, minced

-2 cups vegetable broth

-1 tablespoon low-sodium soy sauce

-1/2 teaspoon red pepper flakes

-1/4 teaspoon ground black pepper

-2 cups fresh vegetables, such as snow peas, mushrooms, carrots, bell peppers, and broccoli

-1 package ramen noodles, whole wheat or gluten-free

Instructions

1. Heat the sesame oil in a large pot over medium heat.

2. Add the ginger and garlic and cook for 1 minute, stirring often.

3. Add the vegetable broth, soy sauce, red pepper flakes, and black pepper and bring to a boil.

4. Reduce the heat to low and add the vegetables. Simmer for 5 minutes.

5. Add the ramen noodles and cook for an additional 5 minutes, or until the noodles are tender.

6. Serve the ramen hot.

Nutritional Value

Calories: 203

Fat: 7.1 g

Carbohydrates: 27.2 g

Protein: 6.2 g

Fiber: 5.9 g

Sugar: 4.1 g

Sesame-Crusted Salmon with Steamed Vegetables

Time Required: 45 minutes

Servings: 4

Ingredients

- 4 (6-ounce) salmon fillets
- 2 tablespoons olive oil
- 2 tablespoons sesame seeds
- 2 teaspoons garlic powder
- 1 teaspoon onion powder
- 1 teaspoon smoked paprika
- 1/2 teaspoon sea salt
- 1/4 teaspoon black pepper
- 2 cups broccoli florets
- 2 cups carrots, sliced
- 2 cups cauliflower florets
- 2 tablespoons butter
- 2 tablespoons freshly-chopped parsley

Instructions

1. Preheat oven to 425°F. Line a baking tray with parchment paper.

2. Place salmon fillets on the baking sheet.

3. In a small bowl, mix olive oil, sesame seeds, garlic powder, onion powder, smoked paprika, sea salt, and black pepper.

4. Brush the mixture over the salmon fillets.

5. Bake for 15 minutes, or until the salmon is cooked through.

6. Meanwhile, bring a large pot of water to a boil.

7. Add the broccoli, carrots, and cauliflower to the boiling water and cook for 5 minutes.

8. Drain the vegetables and transfer to a serving plate.

9. Top the vegetables with butter and parsley.

10. Serve the salmon with the steamed vegetables. Enjoy!

Nutritional Value

Calories - 289

Fat - 15g

Protein - 26g

Carbs - 7g

Fiber - 2g

Sugar - 3g

Sweet and Sour Stir-Fry

Prep time: 10 minutes

Cook time: 10 minutes

Ingredients

- 2 tablespoons olive oil

- 1 red bell pepper, chopped

- 1 green bell pepper, chopped

- 1/2 cup pineapple chunks in natural juice

- 1/2 cup snow peas, chopped

- 1/2 cup bok choy, chopped

- 1/4 cup reduced-sodium soy sauce

- 1 tablespoon honey

- 1 teaspoon cornstarch

- 1/2 teaspoon ground ginger

- 2 cups cooked brown rice

Instructions

1. Heat a large pot over medium-high heat. Add the olive oil and bell peppers and stir-fry for 2 minutes.

2. Add the pineapple and snow peas and stir-fry for 2 minutes. Add the bok choy and stir-fry for 1 minute.

3. In a small bowl, whisk together the soy sauce, honey, cornstarch, and ginger. Pour the sauce over the vegetables and stir to combine.

4. Continue to cook until the vegetables are tender and the sauce has thickened, about 3 minutes.

5. Serve the stir-fry over cooked brown rice.

Nutritional value

Calories: 337

Fat: 7g

Carbohydrates: 55g

Protein: 9g

Sodium: 484mg

Fiber: 7g

Sugar: 11g

Grilled Vegetables over Brown Rice

Prep Time: 10 minutes

Cook Time: 20 minutes

Total Time: 30 minutes

Ingredients

1 cup uncooked brown rice

2 tablespoons olive oil

2 cloves garlic, minced

2 bell peppers, sliced

1 large onion, sliced

1 zucchini, sliced

1 yellow squash, sliced

1/2 teaspoon salt

Instructions

1. Preheat the grill over medium-high heat.

2. Meanwhile, cook the brown rice according to the package instructions.

3. In a large bowl, combine the olive oil, garlic, bell peppers, onion, zucchini, yellow squash, and salt. Toss to combine.

4. Place the vegetables onto the grill and cook for 8-10 minutes, flipping once, until the vegetables are tender and lightly charred.

5. Serve the grilled vegetables over the cooked brown rice.

Nutritional Information (per serving)

Calories: 210

Fat: 7.2g

Carbohydrates: 30.3g

Protein: 4.3g

Fiber: 4.7g

Sodium: 310mg

Japanese-Style Omelette with Vegetables

Time Required: 10 minutes

Ingredients

2 Eggs

1/4 Red Bell Pepper, finely chopped

1/4 Onion, finely chopped

1/4 cup Broccoli, chopped

1/4 cup Mushrooms, chopped

1 teaspoon Sesame Oil

1 teaspoon Soy Sauce

Instructions

1. Heat sesame oil in a non-stick skillet over medium heat.

2. Add bell pepper, onion, broccoli and mushrooms to the skillet and cook for 5 minutes until vegetables are tender.

3. In a separate bowl, whisk together eggs, soy sauce and a pinch of salt.

4. Pour egg mixture into the skillet with vegetables and let cook for 3 minutes until the edges of the omelette are set.

5. Carefully flip the omelette and cook for another 2 minutes until cooked through.

6. Serve hot.

Nutritional Value

Calories: 111

Protein: 7 g

Carbohydrates: 3 g

Fat: 8 g

Fiber: 1 g

Sodium: 244 mg

Steamed Dumplings with Vegetables

Prep Time: 20 minutes

Cook Time: 10 minutes

Total Time: 30 minutes

Servings: 4

Ingredients

- 1/2 cup shredded carrots

- 1/2 cup chopped mushrooms

- 1/2 cup chopped green onion

- 1/2 cup shredded cabbage

- 1 teaspoon sesame oil

- 1 tablespoon reduced-sodium soy sauce

- 1 package wonton wrappers

- 2 tablespoons vegetable oil

Instructions

1. In a large bowl, combine carrots, mushrooms, green onion, cabbage, sesame oil, and soy sauce. Mix until vegetables are evenly coated.

2. Place 1 tablespoon of the vegetable mixture in the center of each wonton wrapper.

3. Wet your finger and run it along the edges of each wrapper. Fold the wrapper in half and press the edges together to form a seal.

4. Line a steamer with parchment paper or a damp cloth. Place the dumplings in the steamer, making sure they don't touch.

5. Place the steamer over boiling water. Cover and cook for 10 minutes or until the dumplings are cooked through.

6. Serve hot with your favorite dipping sauce. Enjoy!

Nutritional Value

Calories: 222

Fat: 5 g

Carbohydrates: 32 g

Protein: 9 g

Korean-Style Beef and Vegetable Stew

Time Required: 25 minutes

Ingredients

-1 tablespoon of olive oil

-1 pound of lean ground beef

-1 large onion, chopped

-3 cloves of garlic, minced

-1 tablespoon of fresh ginger, grated

-1 teaspoon of sesame oil

-2 tablespoons of soy sauce

-1 teaspoon of brown sugar

-1 teaspoon of red pepper flakes

-2 cups of low-sodium beef broth

-1 large sweet potato, peeled and cubed

-1 large carrot, peeled and chopped

-1 cup of frozen peas

-3 green onions, chopped

Directions

1. Heat the olive oil in a large saucepan over medium-high heat.

2. Add the ground beef and cook until the beef is browned, about 5 minutes.

3. Add the onion, garlic, and ginger and cook until the vegetables are softened, about 5 minutes.

4. Add the sesame oil, soy sauce, brown sugar, and red pepper flakes and stir to combine.

5. Pour in the beef broth and bring the mixture to a boil.

6. Reduce the heat to low and add the sweet potato and carrot. Simmer for 10 minutes.

7. Add the frozen peas and cook for an additional 5 minutes.

8. Stir in the green onions and serve.

Nutritional Value

Calories: 255

Fat: 9.7g

Carbohydrates: 19.3g

Protein: 23.2g

Sodium: 550mg

Vegetable Curry

Time required: 45 minutes

Servings: 4

Ingredients

- 1 tablespoon olive oil
- 1 onion, diced
- 2 cloves garlic, minced
- 1 teaspoon ginger, grated
- 1 teaspoon ground cumin
- 1 teaspoon ground coriander
- 1 teaspoon turmeric
- 1 teaspoon garam masala
- 1/4 teaspoon cayenne pepper
- 1/4 teaspoon ground cardamom
- 1 can (14.5 ounces) diced tomatoes
- 1 cup vegetable broth
- 1/2 cup coconut milk
- 2 large potatoes, cubed
- 1 large carrot, sliced
- 1 red bell pepper, diced
- 1/2 cup frozen peas
- 2 tablespoons fresh cilantro, chopped

Instructions

1. Heat the olive oil in a large saucepan over medium heat.

2. Add the onion and garlic and cook until softened, about 5 minutes.

3. Add the ginger, cumin, coriander, turmeric, garam masala, cayenne pepper, and cardamom and cook, stirring, for 1 minute.

4. Add the tomatoes, vegetable broth, and coconut milk and bring to a simmer.

5. Add the potatoes, carrot, and bell pepper and simmer for 15 minutes.

6. Add the peas and simmer for 5 minutes more.

7. Stir in the cilantro and season with salt and pepper, to taste.

8. Serve hot with basmati rice. Enjoy!

Nutritional Value

Calories: 139

Fat: 6 g

Carbohydrates: 18 g

Protein: 5 g

Vegetable Spring Rolls

Time Required: 25 minutes

Ingredients

- 8 ounces firm or extra-firm tofu

- 1 teaspoon olive oil

- 1/2 cup shredded carrots

- 1/2 cup shredded red cabbage

- 1/2 cup bean sprouts

- 8-10 spring roll wrappers

- 2 tablespoons soy sauce

- 2 tablespoons rice vinegar

- 2 tablespoons honey

Instructions

1. Preheat oven to 400°F. Place the tofu on a parchment-lined baking sheet and bake for 15 minutes.

2. Heat the olive oil in a large pot over medium heat. Add the carrots, cabbage, and bean sprouts. Fry for 5 minutes, stirring occasionally.

3. Meanwhile, place one wrapper at a time in a shallow bowl of warm water for about 10 seconds or until it becomes pliable.

4. Place the wrapper on a cutting board. Place a few tablespoons of the vegetables and a few small cubes of tofu at the center of the wrapperZA.

5. Fold in the sides of the wrapper and then roll up. Place the spring roll on a plate and repeat with the remaining wrappers and filling.

6. In a small bowl, mix together the soy sauce, rice vinegar, and honey.

7. Serve the spring rolls with the dipping sauce. Enjoy!

Nutritional Value

Calories: 100

Total Fat: 2g

Sat. Fat: 0g

Carbs: 17g

Protein: 3g

Egg Foo Young

Time Required: 15 minutes

Ingredients

- 3 eggs

- 1 cup of chopped vegetables (onion, peppers, mushrooms, etc)

- 2 tablespoons of low-sodium soy sauce

- 2 tablespoons of cornstarch

- 2 tablespoons of olive oil

- Salt and pepper to taste

Instructions

1. Beat the eggs in a bowl and season with salt and pepper.

2. Heat the olive oil in a large pot over medium heat.

3. Add the vegetables and sauté for about 5 minutes, or until the vegetables are tender.

4. Add the beaten eggs to the skillet and stir to combine.

5. In a small bowl, mix together the soy sauce and cornstarch.

6. Add the soy sauce mixture to the eggs and vegetables and stir until everything is combined.

7. Cook the egg foo young for 5-7 minutes, or until the eggs are cooked through.

8. Serve warm.

Nutritional Value

- Calories: 210

- Fat: 13.5 g

- Carbohydrates: 8.6 g

- Protein: 11.7 g

- Sodium: 531 mg

Grilled Shrimp and Vegetable Skewers

Time Required: 15 minutes

Servings: 4

Ingredients

-1 pound large shrimp, peeled and deveined

-1 red bell pepper, cut into 1-inch cubes

-1 yellow bell pepper, cut into 1-inch cubes

-1 zucchini, cut into 1-inch cubes

-1 red onion, cut into 1-inch cubes

-2 tablespoons olive oil

-1 teaspoon garlic powder

-1 teaspoon chili powder

-1/2 teaspoon paprika

-1/2 teaspoon salt

-1/4 teaspoon black pepper

-4 wooden skewers, soaked in water for 10 minutes

Instructions

1. Preheat your grill to medium-high heat.

2. In a large bowl, combine the shrimp, bell peppers, zucchini, and red onion.

3. Drizzle the olive oil over the vegetables and shrimp and season with garlic powder, chili powder, paprika, salt, and black pepper. Toss to combine.

4. Thread the vegetables and shrimp onto the wooden skewers.

5. Place the skewers on the preheated grill and cook for 7-8 minutes, turning once, or until the shrimp are cooked through and the vegetables are slightly charred.

6. Serve with your favorite side dish and enjoy.

Nutritional Value

Calories: 246

Total Fat: 10.1g

Saturated Fat: 1.8g

Cholesterol: 172mg

Sodium: 246mg

Carbohydrates: 13.2g

Fiber: 3.1g

Protein: 23.5g

Stir-Fried Noodles with Vegetables

Servings: 4

Prep Time: 10 minutes

Cook Time: 15 minutes

Total Time: 25 minutes

Ingredients

- 8 ounces whole wheat noodles

- 2 tablespoons olive oil

- 1 onion, diced

- 2 cloves garlic, minced

- 2 carrots, sliced

- 2 red bell peppers, diced

- 1 head broccoli, cut into florets

- 1/4 cup low-sodium soy sauce

Instructions

1. Cook the noodles according to package directions. Drain and set aside.

2. Heat the olive oil in a large skillet over medium heat. Add the onion and garlic and cook for 2 minutes.

3. Add the carrots, bell peppers, and broccoli and cook for 5 minutes, or until vegetables are tender.

4. Add the cooked noodles and soy sauce and stir to combine. Cook for an additional 5 minutes, stirring occasionally.

5. Serve immediately.

Nutritional Value

Calories: 276

Fat: 7.2g

Carbohydrates: 43.8g

Fiber: 6.9g

Protein: 8.8g

Korean-Style Stir-Fried Glass Noodles

Time Required: 15 minutes

Ingredients

- 2 tablespoons vegetable oil

- 2 cloves of garlic, minced

- 1 cup mushrooms, sliced

- 2 cups baby spinach

- 1/2 cup carrots, julienned

- 4 ounces glass noodles, cooked according to package instructions

- 2 tablespoons soy sauce

- 2 tablespoons sesame oil

- 1/2 teaspoon freshly ground black pepper

Instructions

1. Heat the vegetable oil in a large pot over medium-high heat. Add the garlic and mushrooms and cook for 2 minutes, stirring frequently.

2. Add the spinach, carrots, and noodles and stir-fry for 3 minutes.

3. Add the soy sauce, sesame oil, and black pepper and stir-fry for an additional 2 minutes.

4. Serve hot.

Nutritional Value

Calories: 270

Fat: 15 g

Carbohydrates: 27 g

Protein: 8 g

Fiber: 3 g

Sodium: 890 mg

Vegetable-Filled Steamed Dumplings

Prep Time: 15 minutes

Cook Time: 15 minutes

Total Time: 30 minutes

Servings: 4

Ingredients

-1 package of wonton wrappers

-2 cups chopped vegetables of your choice (such as carrots, celery, peppers, etc.)

-1 tablespoon vegetable oil

-2 cloves of garlic, minced

-1 teaspoon fresh ginger, grated

-2 tablespoons soy sauce

-2 tablespoons sesame oil

-2 tablespoons rice vinegar

-1 teaspoon sugar

Instructions

1. Heat the vegetable oil in a large skillet over medium heat.

2. Add the vegetables and sauté for 5 minutes, or until tender.

3. Add the garlic, ginger, soy sauce, sesame oil, rice vinegar, and sugar. Stir to combine.

4. Remove the skillet from the heat and let the mixture cool completely.

5. To assemble the dumplings, place a wonton wrapper on a work surface. Place 1 teaspoon of the vegetable mixture in the center.

6. Use water to wet the edges of the wonton wrapper. Fold the wrapper in half and press the edges together to seal.

7. Repeat the process with the remaining wrappers and filling.

8. Place the dumplings in a steamer basket, cover and steam over boiling water for 10 minutes.

9. Serve the dumplings warm with additional soy sauce, if desired. Enjoy!

Nutritional Value

Calories: 112

Fat: 1g

Carbohydrates: 19g

Protein: 4g

Fiber: 3g

Tofu and Vegetable Stir-Fry

Ingredients

- 1 tsp olive oil

- 1 block extra firm tofu, drained and cubed

- 2 cloves garlic, minced

- 1 red bell pepper, sliced

- 1 cup broccoli florets

- 1/2 cup mushrooms, sliced

- 1/4 cup low-sodium soy sauce

- 1 tsp sesame oil

- 1/4 tsp ground ginger

Instructions

1. Heat oil in a large non-stick skillet over medium-high heat.

2. Add the tofu and cook for 5 minutes, stirring occasionally.

3. Add garlic, bell pepper, broccoli, mushrooms, soy sauce, sesame oil, and ginger. Cook for 5 minutes, stirring occasionally.

4. Reduce heat to low and cook for an additional 5 minutes, stirring occasionally.

5. Serve over hot cooked rice or quinoa.

Nutritional Value (per serving)

Calories: 170

Total Fat: 8g

Saturated Fat: 1g

Cholesterol: 0mg

Sodium: 590mg

Total Carbohydrate: 11g

Dietary Fiber: 3g

Sugars: 4g

Protein: 12g

Vegetarian Sushi Rolls with Cucumber and Avocado

Prep Time: 20 minutes

Cook Time: 10 minutes

Total Time: 30 minutes

Servings: 4 rolls

Ingredients

- 4 sheets nori
- 2 cups cooked sushi rice
- 1 cucumber, cut into matchsticks
- 1 avocado, thinly sliced

- 4 teaspoons reduced-sodium soy sauce

Instructions

1. Place one sheet of nori on a sushi rolling mat.

2. Spread a thin layer of cooked sushi rice over the nori, leaving a 1-inch border on one end.

3. Place cucumber and avocado strips in a line across the middle of the nori.

4. Lift the edge of the mat closest to you and begin to roll the sushi away from you, using your fingers to keep the filling in place.

5. When you reach the end, wet the remaining edge of the nori with a damp towel and press it to the roll to seal.

6. Slice the roll into 6-8 pieces and set aside.

7. Repeat with remaining sheets of nori, sushi rice, and cucumber and avocado.

8. Serve the sushi with soy sauce for dipping. Enjoy!

Desserts

Diabetes is a condition in which the body has difficulty regulating blood sugar levels. While there are many dietary strategies that may help manage diabetes, some individuals may find it difficult to maintain a balanced diet due to cultural preferences and food availability. Thankfully, there are a variety of diabetes-friendly Asian desserts that can be enjoyed in moderation to satisfy sweet cravings without raising blood sugar levels. One of the best Asian desserts for diabetics is mochi. This traditional Japanese treat is made from pounded sweet rice and is usually filled with a sweet bean paste or fruit.

Mochi is low in calories, fat, and carbohydrates, making it an ideal snack for diabetics. It also contains a small amount of fiber and is a source of protein, which helps to slow digestion and reduce blood sugar spikes. Additionally, mochi is naturally gluten-free, making it a great dessert for people with gluten sensitivities. Another great option for diabetics is Bingsu, a Korean shaved ice dessert. Bingsu is typically made with a base of either milk or fruit-flavored syrup and topped with ice and various ingredients such as fruit, nuts, and sweetened condensed milk. Because the syrup and toppings are usually low in sugar, Bingsu can be enjoyed without worrying about blood sugar spikes.

Additionally, the ice can help to lower body temperature, which can be beneficial for diabetics who are prone to overheating. Chinese almond jelly is another great Asian dessert for diabetics. This dessert is usually made with agar-agar, a gelatinous substance derived from seaweed, and is usually flavored with almond extract. Almond jelly is low in sugar and calories, making it an ideal snack for diabetics. Moreover, it is high in fiber and protein, which can help to slow digestion and reduce blood sugar spikes. For diabetics who have a sweet tooth, there are many Asian desserts that can be enjoyed in moderation.

Mochi, Bingsu, and almond jelly are all great options that are low in sugar and calories, and are high in fiber and protein. By eating these desserts in moderation, diabetics can satisfy their cravings without worrying about blood sugar spikes.

Coconut Jello

Servings: 6

Prep Time: 10 minutes

Cook Time: 5 minutes

Total Time: 15 minutes

Ingredients

-1 (14 ounce) can light coconut milk

-2.5 tablespoons unflavored gelatin

-2 tablespoons honey

-2 tablespoons shredded coconut

-¼ teaspoon coconut extract

Instructions

1. In a medium saucepan, heat the coconut milk over medium heat until it comes to a gentle simmer.

2. Reduce the heat to low and stir in the gelatin, honey, shredded coconut and coconut extract until everything is fully incorporated.

3. Remove the saucepan from the heat and pour the mixture into a 9-inch round baking dish.

4. Refrigerate for at least four hours or until completely set.

Nutritional Value

Calories: 92

Fat: 5g

Carbohydrates: 11g

Protein: 2g

Fiber: 1g

Sugar: 9g

Coconut Rice Pudding

Total Time: 35 minutes

Servings: 6

Ingredients

- 1 cup uncooked long-grain white rice
- 1/4 teaspoon salt
- 2 cups low-fat milk
- 1/4 cup sugar
- 1/2 teaspoon ground cinnamon
- 1/4 teaspoon ground nutmeg
- 1/2 cup flaked coconut
- 2 tablespoons butter
- 1 teaspoon vanilla extract

Instructions

1. Preheat oven to 350°F.

2. In a medium saucepan, bring 1 1/2 cups of water, the rice, and salt to a boil. Reduce heat to low, cover, and simmer for 20 minutes or until the rice is tender.

3. In a medium bowl, combine the cooked rice, milk, sugar, cinnamon, nutmeg, coconut, butter, and vanilla extract.

4. Transfer the mixture to a 9-inch baking dish. Bake for 15 minutes or until the pudding is bubbly.

5. Serve warm.

Nutritional Value per Serving

Calories: 204

Carbohydrates: 33g

Protein: 4g

Fat: 6g

Red Bean Soup

Serving size: 1 cup

Time required: 25 minutes

Ingredients

- 1 tablespoon olive oil

- 1 onion, diced

- 2 cloves garlic, minced

- 2 carrots, peeled and diced

- 2 stalks celery, diced

- 1 teaspoon chili powder

- 1 teaspoon ground cumin

- 5 cups vegetable broth

- 2 cans (15 ounces each) red beans, rinsed and drained

- Salt and pepper to taste

Instructions

1. Heat the olive oil in a large pot over medium-high heat.

2. Add the onion, garlic, carrots, and celery and sauté until the vegetables are softened and the onion is translucent, about 5 minutes.

3. Add the chili powder and cumin and cook for another minute.

4. Add the vegetable broth and bring to a boil.

5. Add the beans and reduce heat to low. Simmer for 15 minutes.

6. Remove from heat and use an immersion blender to blend the soup until smooth.

7. Season to taste.

Nutritional Value

Calories: 112

Fat: 3.2 g

Carbohydrates: 18 g

Protein: 4.7 g

Fiber: 5.3 g

Sugar: 2.3 g

Mango Pudding

Time Required: 10 minutes

Ingredients

- 1 ripe mango, peeled and cut into small pieces

- 2 tablespoons of sugar-free sweetener

- 2 tablespoons of cornstarch

- 2 cups of unsweetened almond milk

- ½ teaspoon of vanilla extract

Instructions

1. In a medium saucepan, combine the mango pieces and the sugar-free sweetener. Bring to a gentle boil and cook for 2 minutes, stirring occasionally.

2. Reduce the heat to low and add the cornstarch and the almond milk, whisking until the mixture thickens and the cornstarch is fully dissolved.

3. Remove from the heat and stir in the vanilla extract.

4. Transfer the pudding to a bowl and let it cool slightly before serving.

Nutritional Value

Calories: 128

Fat: 3g

Carbohydrates: 24g

Protein: 2g

Fiber: 2g

Sugar: 17g

Sweet Potato Pie

Ingredients

- 3 cups mashed sweet potatoes

- ½ cup light brown sugar

- ¼ cup honey

- 2 eggs

- ½ cup low-fat milk

- 1 teaspoon cinnamon

- 1 teaspoon nutmeg

- 1 teaspoon vanilla extract

- 1 unbaked 9-inch pie crust

Directions

1. Preheat oven to 375 degrees.

2. In a large bowl, mash sweet potatoes and brown sugar until smooth.

3. Add honey, eggs, milk, cinnamon, nutmeg, and vanilla extract. Mix until completely combined.

4. Pour mixture into unbaked 9-inch pie crust.

5. Bake for 40-45 minutes.

6. Allow pie to cool before serving.

Nutritional Value (per serving)

Calories: 150

Fat: 5 g

Carbohydrates: 23 g

Protein: 4 g

Sugar: 14 g

Fiber: 3 g

Tapioca Pudding

Prep time: 10 minutes

Cook time: 10 minutes

Total time: 20 minutes

Ingredients

-1/4 cup tapioca pearls

-1/4 teaspoon salt

-2 tablespoons granulated sugar

-2 1/2 cups fat-free milk

-1 teaspoon vanilla extract

-1 tablespoon butter

-Cinnamon and nutmeg to taste

Directions

1. In a medium saucepan, bring 3 cups of water to a boil.

2. Add the tapioca pearls and salt, and stir to combine. Reduce the heat to medium-low and simmer for 10 minutes, stirring occasionally.

3. Add the sugar, milk, vanilla, and butter to the pot and stir to combine. Simmer for another 10 minutes, stirring occasionally.

4. Remove the pot from the heat and let cool for 5 minutes.

5. Serve the pudding warm or cold, sprinkled with cinnamon and nutmeg to taste.

Nutritional Value (per serving)

Calories: 207

Fat: 7g

Carbohydrates: 32g

Protein: 5g

Fiber: 1g

Sugar: 18g

Sodium: 199mg

Green Tea Ice Cream

Ingredients

2 cups of skim milk

2 tablespoons of green tea powder

2 tablespoons of stevia

1/2 teaspoon of vanilla extract

Instructions

1. In a medium-sized bowl, combine the skim milk and green tea powder.

2. Mix together until the powder is completely dissolved.

3. Add the stevia and vanilla extract and mix until combined.

4. Place the mixture in the refrigerator for 2 hours.

5. Once chilled, pour the mixture into an ice cream maker and churn according to the manufacturer's instructions.

6. Freeze for 4-6 hours before serving.

Nutritional Value (per 1/2 cup serving)

Calories: 51,

Fat: 0.3g,

Carbohydrates: 8.3g,

Protein: 2.3g.

Rice Pudding with Sesame Seeds

Time Required: 30 minutes

Servings: 4

Ingredients

- 2 cups cooked brown rice

- 2 cups low-fat milk

- 2 tablespoons honey or natural sugar substitute

- 2 tablespoons sesame seeds

- 1 teaspoon ground cinnamon

- 1/4 teaspoon ground nutmeg

- 1/4 teaspoon ground cardamom

Instructions

1. Oven should be preheated to 350 degrees F.

2. In a medium bowl, combine cooked rice, milk, honey, sesame seeds, cinnamon, nutmeg, and cardamom.

3. Pour mixture into a greased 9-inch pie plate.

4. Bake for 30 minutes, or until pudding is set and golden brown.

5. Serve warm or chilled. Enjoy!

Nutritional Value

Calories: 260

Total Fat: 6.5 g

Saturated Fat: 1.8 g

Cholesterol: 0 m

Sodium: 94 mg

Carbohydrates: 45 g

Fiber: 2.8 g

Protein: 5.4 g

Sesame Balls

Prep time: 30 minutes

Cook time: 15 minutes

Total time: 45 minutes

Servings: 12 balls

Ingredients

- 1/2 cup sesame seeds

- 2 tablespoons maple syrup
- 1/2 teaspoon ground cinnamon
- 1/4 cup almond flour
- 1/4 cup coconut flour

- 2 tablespoons coconut oil, melted
- 1/4 teaspoon sea salt

Instructions

1. Preheat oven to 350°F (180°C) and line a baking sheet with parchment paper.

2. In a bowl, mix together sesame seeds, maple syrup, and cinnamon until combined.

3. In a separate bowl, mix together almond flour, coconut flour, melted coconut oil, and sea salt until combined.

4. Add wet ingredients to the dry ingredients and mix until a dough forms.

5. Using your hands, form 12 balls with the dough and place on the baking sheet.

6. Bake for 15 minutes until golden brown.

7. Allow to cool before serving. Enjoy!

Nutritional Value (per ball)

Calories: 80

Carbohydrates: 10g

Protein: 1.5g

Fat: 4g

Almond Cookies

Prep Time: 10 minutes

Cook Time: 10 minutes

Total Time: 20 minutes

Yield: 15-20 cookies

Ingredients

- 1 cup almond flour
- 1/4 cup coconut sugar
- 1/4 teaspoon sea salt
- 1/4 teaspoon baking soda
- 1/4 cup butter, melted
- 1 teaspoon vanilla extract
- 1/4 cup sliced almonds

Instructions

1. Preheat the oven to 350°F.

2. In a medium bowl, mix together the almond flour, coconut sugar, sea salt, and baking soda.

3. In a separate bowl, whisk together the melted butter and vanilla extract.

4. Add the wet ingredients to the dry ingredients and mix until fully combined.

5. Using a spoon or cookie scoop, scoop out 1 tablespoon of the cookie dough and roll into a ball. Place on a parchment-lined baking sheet.

6. Press the cookie dough ball down slightly with your palm, and top with a few sliced almonds.

7. Bake for 10 minutes, or until golden brown.

8. Let cool on the baking sheet for a few minutes before transferring to a cooling rack to cool completely. Enjoy!

Nutritional Value

- Calories: 125
- Fat: 8g
- Carbohydrates: 9g
- Protein: 3g

Matcha Pancakes

Time Required: 25 minutes

Servings: 4

Ingredients

- 1 cup whole wheat flour

1 teaspoon baking powder

1 teaspoon matcha powder

1/4 teaspoon sea salt

2 large eggs

1 cup unsweetened almond milk

2 tablespoons extra-virgin olive oil

Instructions

1. In a medium bowl, whisk together the flour, baking powder, matcha powder and sea salt.

2. In a separate bowl, whisk together the eggs, almond milk and olive oil until well combined.

3. Pour the wet ingredients into the dry ingredients and whisk until just combined.

4. Heat a non-stick skillet over medium-high heat and lightly grease with a bit of olive oil.

5. Drop 1/4 cup of the batter onto the skillet and cook until golden brown and cooked through.

6. Flip and cook the other side until golden brown.

7. Repeat with remaining batter.

8. Serve pancakes with your favorite topping such as fresh berries or pure maple syrup. Enjoy!

Nutritional Value (per serving)

Calories: 250

Protein: 8g

Carbs: 30g

Fat: 10g

Steamed Buns with Sweet Bean Filling

Time Required: 30 minutes

Ingredients

-1 cup sweet bean paste

-1/2 cup all-purpose flour

- 1/2 cup whole wheat flour

- 2 tablespoons vegetable oil

- 1/4 teaspoon baking powder

- 1/4 teaspoon salt

- 1/2 cup warm water

Instructions

1. In a large bowl, mix together the all-purpose flour, whole wheat flour, vegetable oil, baking powder, and salt.

2. Gradually add in the warm water, mixing until a soft, dough forms.

3. Knead the dough for 3-4 minutes, until it is smooth and elastic.

4. Divide the dough into 8 equal pieces and roll each piece into a ball.

5. Place each ball of dough on a lightly floured surface and use a rolling pin to flatten each ball into a round shape.

6. Place 1 tablespoon of

7. Fold the dough over the filling and press the edges together to seal.

8. Place the buns on a lightly greased steamer tray.

9. Steam for about 15 minutes, or until the buns are cooked through.

10. Serve warm. Enjoy!

Nutritional Value

Calories: 152

Carbohydrates: 28g

Protein: 4g

Fat: 2g

Chinese Egg Custard - Diabetes-Friendly Recipe

Servings: 4

Time Required: 40 minutes

Ingredients

- 4 eggs

- 2 cups of low-fat milk

- 1/4 cup of cornstarch

- 2 tablespoons of sugar

- 1 teaspoon of salt

- 2 tablespoons of olive oil

- 1 teaspoon of sesame oil

- 2 tablespoons of green onions, finely chopped

- 1/4 cup of mushrooms, finely chopped

Instructions

1. Oven should be preheated to 325 degrees F (165 degrees C).

2. In a medium bowl, whisk together eggs, milk, cornstarch, sugar, and salt until well combined.

3. Heat olive oil in a medium skillet over medium heat.

4. Add green onions and mushrooms and cook until softened, about 5 minutes.

5. Add egg mixture to skillet, stirring constantly.

6. Cook until mixture is thick, about 8 minutes.

7. Pour egg mixture into a greased 9-inch pie plate.

8. Drizzle sesame oil over the top.

9. Bake in preheated oven for 25 minutes, or until custard is set.

10. Cool for 10 minutes before serving.

Nutritional Value

196 calories

7.2 g of fat

20.2 g of carbohydrates

13.1 g of protein

Fried Banana Roll

Prep Time: 10 minutes

Cook Time: 5 minutes

Total Time: 15 minutes

Ingredients

- 1 banana

- 2 tablespoons of peanut butter

- 2 tablespoons of ground flaxseed

- 1 teaspoon of honey

- 2 tablespoons of coconut oil

Directions

1. Peel and slice the banana into 1/2 inch thick slices.

2. Spread the peanut butter, ground flaxseed, and honey on top of each banana slice.

3. Heat the coconut oil in a skillet over medium heat.

4. Place each banana slice in the skillet and cook for 2-3 minutes on each side or until lightly browned.

5. Transfer the banana rolls to a plate and serve.

Nutritional Value

Calories: 204

Fat: 15 g

Carbohydrates: 15 g

Protein: 4 g

Fiber: 4 g

Sugar: 8 g

Fried Dough Sticks

Time Required: 25 minutes

Ingredients

-1 cup all-purpose flour

-1/2 teaspoon salt

-1 teaspoon baking powder

-2 tablespoons olive oil

- 1/2 cup warm water

- 1/4 cup vegetable oil, for frying

Instructions

1. In a large bowl, combine the flour, salt, and baking powder.

2. Add the olive oil and warm water, and mix until a soft dough forms.

3. Turn the dough out onto a floured surface and knead it for 5 minutes.

4. Roll the dough out into a thin sheet, about 1/4-inch thick.

5. Cut the dough into strips about 1/2-inch wide and 4-inches long.

6. Heat the vegetable oil in a large skillet over medium-high heat.

7. Fry the dough strips in batches, until golden brown and crispy.

8. Transfer to a plate lined with paper towels to drain any excess oil.

9. Serve warm.

Nutritional Value

Calories: 204

Fat: 10.7 g

Carbohydrates: 21.5 g

Protein: 3.3 g

Fiber: 0.8 g

Caramelized Apples

Time Required: 15 minutes

Servings: 4

Ingredients

- 4 medium apples, cored and sliced
- 4 teaspoons butter, melted
- 4 tablespoons brown sugar
- 1 teaspoon ground cinnamon
- Pinch of ground nutmeg
- Pinch of sea salt

Instructions

1. Oven should be preheated to 375 degrees F.

2. Place the apple slices in a single layer on a baking sheet.

3. Drizzle the melted butter over the apple slices and sprinkle with the brown sugar, cinnamon, nutmeg, and salt.

4. Bake for 10 minutes, then remove from the oven and flip the apples over.

5. Return to the oven and bake for an additional 5 minutes, or until the apples are golden brown and tender.

6. Serve warm.

Nutritional Value

Calories: 93 kcal

Fat: 0.5 g

Carbohydrates: 24 g

Protein: 0.5 g

Baked Sweet Potatoes

Prep Time: 10 minutes

Cook Time: 45 minutes

Total Time: 55 minutes

Servings: 2

Ingredients

- 2 large sweet potatoes

- 2 tablespoons olive oil

- 1 teaspoon garlic powder

- 1 teaspoon onion powder

- 1 teaspoon paprika

- 1/2 teaspoon salt

- 1/4 teaspoon black pepper

Instructions

1. Oven should be preheated to 375 degrees F.

2. Wash potatoes and pat dry.

3. Slice potatoes into 1/2 inch thick slices.

4. Place slices on a baking sheet and brush with olive oil.

5. Sprinkle garlic powder, onion powder, paprika, salt, and pepper over potatoes.

6. Bake in preheated oven for 45 minutes, flipping slices halfway through.

7. Serve warm and enjoy!

Nutritional Value

Calories: 135.5

Fat: 0.0 g

Carbohydrates: 32.2 g

Protein: 2.2 g

Baked Sweet Potato Balls

Time Required: 30 minutes

Servings: 8

Ingredients

-2 large sweet potatoes

-1/4 cup all-purpose flour

-1/4 cup almond flour

-1 teaspoon baking powder

-1/4 teaspoon ground cinnamon

-1/8 teaspoon ground nutmeg

-1/2 teaspoon sea salt

-1/4 cup maple syrup

-2 tablespoons melted coconut oil

-1 teaspoon vanilla extract

Instructions

1. Preheat the oven to 375°F and line a baking sheet with parchment paper.

2. Peel and chop the sweet potatoes. Place them in a pot, cover with water, and bring to a boil. Boil for 10 minutes or until fork-tender. Drain and mash with a potato masher.

3. In a medium bowl, stir together the all-purpose flour, almond flour, baking powder, cinnamon, nutmeg, and salt.

4. In a separate bowl, whisk together the maple syrup, coconut oil and vanilla extract.

5. Add the wet ingredients to the dry ingredients and stir until combined.

6. Add the mashed sweet potatoes and stir until combined.

7. Using a cookie scoop, scoop the sweet potato mixture and form into balls. Place the balls on the prepared baking sheet and bake for 15 minutes.

8. Serve warm and enjoy!

Nutritional Value

Calories: 97

Fat: 0.4 g

Carbohydrates: 21.3 g

Protein: 1.8 g

Fruit Compote

Ingredients

- 2 cups of fresh or frozen berries of your choice
- ½ cup of sugar-free orange juice
- 2 tablespoons of chia seeds
- 2 tablespoons of lemon juice
- 2 tablespoons of honey

Instructions

1. In a medium-sized saucepan, combine the berries, orange juice, chia seeds, lemon juice, and honey.

2. Bring to a boil over medium-high heat, stirring constantly.

3. Reduce the heat to low and simmer for 10 minutes, stirring occasionally.

4. Remove from the heat and let cool for 5 minutes.

5. Serve warm or chilled.

Nutritional Value

Calories: 97 kcal

Carbohydrates: 17.4 g

Fiber: 5.8 g

Protein: 2.2 g

Fat: 2.8 g

Date-Walnut Cake

Total Time: 45 minutes

Prep Time: 10 minutes

Cook Time: 35 minutes

Ingredients

-1 ½ cups all-purpose flour

-1 teaspoon baking soda

-1 teaspoon baking powder

-½ teaspoon salt

-1 cup chopped dates

-1 cup chopped walnuts

-1 cup applesauce

-2 tablespoons olive oil

- 1 cup sugar

- 1 teaspoon vanilla extract

Instructions

1. Preheat oven to 350°F. Grease and flour a 9" round cake pan.

2. In a medium bowl, combine the flour, baking soda, baking powder, and salt.

3. In another bowl, combine the dates, walnuts, applesauce, olive oil, sugar, and vanilla extract.

4. Add the dry ingredients to the wet ingredients and mix until just combined.

5. Pour the batter into the prepared pan and bake for 30-35 minutes, or until a toothpick inserted comes out clean.

6. Let cool before slicing and serving.

Nutritional Value

Serving Size: 1 slice

Calories: 166

Fat: 6.7g

Carbohydrates: 24g

Protein: 2.7g

Fiber: 1.7g

Sugars: 13g

Baked Apples with Cinnamon

Time Required: 30 minutes

Servings: 4

Ingredients

4 apples, cored

1/4 cup brown sugar

1 teaspoon ground cinnamon

1/4 teaspoon ground nutmeg

1/4 cup water

Instructions

1. Oven should be to 350°F.

2. Place apples in an 8-inch baking dish.

3. In a small bowl, mix together the brown sugar, cinnamon, and nutmeg.

4. Sprinkle the mixture over the apples.

5. Pour the water into the dish.

6. Cover the dish with foil and bake for 25 minutes.

7. Remove the foil and bake for an additional 5 minutes.

7. Serve warm. Enjoy!

Nutritional Value (per serving)

Calories: 133

Fat: 0.4 g

Carbohydrates: 33.1g

Protein: 0.3g

Baked Sweet Potato Mash

Total Time: 35 minutes

Ingredients

- 2 large sweet potatoes, peeled and cubed

- 2 tablespoons olive oil

- 2 cloves garlic, minced

- 2 tablespoons chopped fresh parsley

- 1/2 teaspoon dried thyme

- Salt and pepper, to taste

Instructions

1. Oven should be preheated to 425°F (220°C).

2. Arrange the sweet potato cubes on a baking sheet lined with parchment paper.

3. Drizzle with olive oil, and season with garlic, parsley, thyme, salt, and pepper.

4. Bake for 25 minutes or until the potatoes are tender.

5. Transfer the potatoes to a large bowl and mash with a potato masher until desired consistency is reached.

6. Serve hot.

Nutritional Information (per serving)

Calories: 160

Fat: 7g

Carbohydrates: 22g

Protein: 2g

Fiber: 2g

Fried Tofu with Syrup

Time required: 30 minutes

Ingredients

- 1 package of firm tofu, drained and pressed
- 1/4 cup all-purpose flour
- 1/4 teaspoon garlic powder
- 1/4 teaspoon onion powder
- 1/4 teaspoon black pepper
- 1/4 cup olive oil
- 1/4 cup maple syrup

Instructions

1. Slice the tofu into 1/2-inch cubes.

2. In a shallow bowl, mix together the flour, garlic powder, onion powder, and black pepper.

3. Toss the tofu cubes in the flour mixture, making sure they are evenly coated.

4. Heat the olive oil in a large pan over medium heat.

5. Add the coated tofu cubes to the pan and fry them until they are golden brown, about 6 minutes.

6. Remove the tofu cubes from the pan and place them on a paper towel-lined plate.

8. Drizzle the maple syrup over the tofu cubes and serve immediately. Enjoy!

Nutritional value (per serving)

Calories: 149

Fat: 6.2 g

Carbohydrates: 14.9 g

Protein: 8.2 g

Fried Taro Balls

Time Required: 40 minutes

Ingredients

- 1 ½ cups taro root, grated

- 1 tablespoon of olive oil

- 1 teaspoon of ground black pepper

- ½ teaspoon of garlic powder

- ¼ teaspoon of cumin

- ¼ teaspoon of sea salt

- ¼ cup of all-purpose flour

Instructions

1. Preheat the oven to 375°F.

2. In a medium bowl, combine grated taro, olive oil, black pepper, garlic powder, cumin, and sea salt.

3. Mix until the ingredients are evenly distributed.

4. Form into 1-inch balls and place on a baking sheet lined with parchment paper.

5. Bake for 25 minutes, flipping halfway through.

6. After baking, roll the balls in the flour until evenly coated.

7. Heat a pan over medium heat and add enough oil to lightly coat the bottom of the pan.

8. Fry the taro balls for 5 minutes, flipping halfway through.

9. Remove the balls from the pan and drain on a paper towel.

10. Serve with your favorite dipping sauce or enjoy as is.

Nutritional Value

- Calories: 187

- Fat: 7.1 g

- Carbohydrates: 28.8 g

- Protein: 2.9 g

- Fiber: 2.1 g

- Sugar: 1.3 g

Black Bean Soup

Time Required: 30 minutes

Servings: 4

Ingredients

-2 teaspoons olive oil

-1 onion, chopped

-3 cloves garlic, minced

-2 teaspoons chili powder

-1 teaspoon cumin

-1/4 teaspoon cayenne pepper

-3 cups vegetable broth

-2 (15-ounce) cans black beans, rinsed and drained

-1 (14.5-ounce) can diced tomatoes, undrained

-Salt and pepper to taste

-Fresh cilantro for garnish (optional)

Instructions

1. Heat the oil in a large pot over medium heat.

2. Add the onion and garlic and cook until softened, about 5 minutes.

3. Add the chili powder, cumin and cayenne pepper and cook for 1 minute.

4. Add the vegetable broth, black beans and tomatoes. Bring to a boil, then reduce heat to low and simmer for 15 minutes.

5. Using an immersion blender, blend the soup until smooth.

6. Taste and adjust seasoning with salt and pepper.

7. Serve hot, garnished with cilantro if desired. Enjoy!

Nutritional Value

Calories: 250,

Fat: 1g,

Carbohydrates: 44g,

Protein: 14g

Sweet Red Bean Soup

Prep Time: 10 minutes

Cook Time: 30 minutes

Ingredients

- 1 cup dry red beans

- 6 cups vegetable broth

- 1 large onion, chopped

- 2 cloves garlic, minced

- 2 tablespoons olive oil

- ½ teaspoon ground cumin

- ¼ teaspoon oregano

- 1 teaspoon salt

- 2 tablespoons honey

- 1 teaspoon ground cinnamon

- 2 tablespoons chopped fresh cilantro

Instructions

1. Soak the red beans in a large bowl of water overnight.

2. Heat the olive oil in a large pot at medium-high heat. Add the onion and garlic and sauté for about 5 minutes, until the onion is softened.

3. Add the vegetable broth and the soaked and drained red beans to the pot.

4. Add the cumin, oregano, and salt and stir to combine.

5. Bring the mixture to a boil, then reduce the heat and simmer, covered, for about 20 minutes, or until the beans are tender.

6. Add the honey and cinnamon and simmer for an additional 5 minutes.

7. Serve the soup topped with fresh cilantro.

Nutritional Value

Calories: 171

Fat: 5.5 g

Carbohydrates: 24 g

Protein: 7.5 g

Fiber: 6 g

Sugar: 7 g

Sodium: 690 mg

Sesame-Honey Glazed Apples

Servings: 4

Prep Time: 10 minutes

Cook Time: 10 minutes

Total Time: 20 minutes

Ingredients

- 2 tablespoons sesame oil

- 4 apples (such as Honeycrisp, Granny Smith, etc.), peeled, cored and sliced into thin wedges

- 1/4 cup honey

- 2 tablespoons lime juice

- 2 tablespoons sesame seeds

- Pinch of salt

Instructions

1. Heat the sesame oil in a large skillet over medium heat.

2. Add the apples and cook, stirring occasionally, until they start to soften and brown, about 8 minutes.

3. Add the honey, lime juice, sesame seeds, and salt and stir to combine.

4. Cook until the apples are tender and the glaze is thickened and sticky, about 2 minutes.

5. Serve warm.

Nutritional Value (Per Serving)

Calories: 155

Carbohydrates: 28g

Protein: 1g

Fat: 5g

Saturated Fat: 1g

Sodium: 8mg

Fiber: 3g

Sugar: 22g

Baked Rice Cake

Time Required: 45 minutes

Servings: 6

Ingredients

-1 cup white long grain rice

-1/2 teaspoon salt

- 2 tablespoons olive oil

- 1/4 cup sugar

- 1/4 cup raisins

- 1 teaspoon ground cinnamon

Instructions

1. Preheat oven to 350°F.

2. Grease a 9-inch baking dish with the olive oil.

3. In a small saucepan, bring 2 cups of water to a boil.

4. Add the rice and salt, reduce the heat to low, cover and simmer for 15 minutes.

5. Remove from heat and stir in the sugar and raisins.

6. Pour the mixture into the prepared baking dish.

7. Sprinkle with the cinnamon.

8. Bake for 30 minutes, or until the rice is golden brown.

9. Serve warm. Enjoy!

Nutritional Value

Calories: 198

Carbs: 37 g

Protein: 4 g

Fat: 2 g

Sweet Rice Cakes

Time Required: 30 minutes

Servings: 8

Ingredients

- 2 cups cooked white basmati rice
- 2 tablespoons sugar
- 2 tablespoons honey
- 2 tablespoons vegetable oil
- ½ teaspoon ground cinnamon
- ½ teaspoon ground cardamom
- ½ cup raisins
- ¼ cup chopped almonds
- 2 tablespoons flaxseed meal

Instructions

1. Preheat oven to 350°F.

2. In a large bowl, combine cooked rice, sugar, honey, vegetable oil, cinnamon, cardamom, raisins, almonds, and flaxseed meal. Mix until thoroughly combined.

3. Grease an 8x8 baking dish and spread the mixture evenly over the bottom.

4. Bake for 25-30 minutes, until the top is golden brown.

5. Allow to cool before serving. Enjoy!

Nutritional Value

Calories: 151

Carbohydrates: 28 g

Fat: 1 g

Protein: 2 g

Chinese Sesame Balls

Time Required: 30 minutes

Serving Size: 4 sesame balls

Ingredients

- 2 cups glutinous rice flour

- 1/4 cup boiling water

- 1/4 cup sesame seeds

- 1/4 cup sugar

- 2 tablespoons vegetable oil

- Oil, for frying

Instructions

1. In a medium bowl, combine the glutinous rice flour, boiling water, sesame seeds, sugar, and vegetable oil. Mix together until a sticky dough forms.

2. Roll the dough into small balls, about 1-inch in diameter.

3. Heat oil in a large pot or wok over medium-high heat.

4. Fry the sesame balls in batches, stirring occasionally, until golden brown and crispy.

5. Remove the balls with a slotted spoon and place on a paper towel lined plate to drain.

6. Serve warm.

Nutritional Value

Calories: 162

Total Fat: 7 g

Saturated Fat: 1 g

Cholesterol: 0 mg

Sodium: 5 mg

Carbohydrates: 23 g

Fiber: 1 g

Sugar: 7 g

Protein: 3 g

Conclusion

The Asian Cookbook for Diabetics is a valuable resource for anyone looking to manage their diabetes through a healthier diet. The recipes featured in the book are easy to follow and provide great flavor, nutrition and variety. The book also provides helpful information on food safety, nutrition and meal planning, as well as tips on how to eat healthy and prepare meals.

The Asian Cookbook for Diabetics is an invaluable resource for anyone looking for creative ways to manage their diabetes. With the guidance of this book, diabetics can easily take control of their diet and make healthy, delicious meals that are also good for their blood sugar. With a wide variety of recipes to choose from, it is easy to find something that is both healthy and tasty. This book is a great addition to any kitchen and will help individuals to enjoy their meals while also staying healthy.

Printed in Dunstable, United Kingdom

71499639R00131